Presented to:

Mr VILLALOBOS . Sr

From:

Date:

MAY. 9th 2018

15 14 13 12   10 9 8 7 6 5 4 3 2 1

Taking a Minute

ISBN: 978-160683-416-9

Copyright © 2012 by Jason Anderson

Published by Harrison House Publishers, Inc.

TAKING A MINUTE

BY

JASON ANDERSON

Harrison House
Tulsa, Oklahoma

New Year Resolutions

It's another year—another brand new year. What are you going to do this year? Every New Year, most people make resolutions focusing on what they are going to quit. For example, I'm finally going to quit eating fast food (ha ha!) We all get focused on what we need to *stop* doing. Forget that for a second, and let me ask you.... what are you going to *start* this year? To be a finisher in life, you have to first start. If you don't start something new, then next New Year's you will be exactly where you are today. So what are you starting? I wanted to go for a drive the other day, but my car would not carry me anywhere until I started it. Your life will not carry you anywhere until you start it. Put the key, which is God's Word, into your heart and turn your life over. God has a plan for you. He wants to direct your footsteps, but He cannot direct feet that are standing still. You can't steer a bike unless it's moving. So get started. Try starting college, a business, or that book you've been wanting to write. Maybe you're making a decision to find a church that you will join or find God—whatever it is, say it loud, and get going.

Nehemiah's Choice

There once was a guy named Nehemiah who was a cupbearer to the Persian king. One day, news came to him that the holy city of Jerusalem was in ruins. Well, to make a long story even longer, Nehemiah took it upon himself to go and rebuild the city wall. Jerusalem was a big, big city with lots and lots of wall, and Nehemiah knew he would need money, workers, and some time off from his regular job to do this work. So he asked his boss, who happened to be the king, if he could go to Jerusalem to rebuild the wall and he asked for some supplies and help to do the job. The king agreed to all of Nehemiah's requests. Let me point out something here. Being cupbearer to the king was a cushy palace job. Nehemiah could sleep in, chill at the palace, enjoy great food—everything around him was beautiful. The job was not hard—he had to pick up a cup and take it to the king, probably three or four times a day. Yet when Nehemiah heard about the need in Jerusalem to rebuild the wall, he decided to leave palace life for sweaty, dirty, hard work. Nehemiah chose to be uncomfortable, to make his life harder in order to do what was right. I think sometimes we are searching to be more comfortable; we want cushy palace life. But Nehemiah shows us the importance of stepping out of what is comfortable and easy, to do something big in life. Something bigger than ourselves. Greatness is going to require hard work and risk. So it's your choice—come on in and take a load off and do nothing, or do something great!

Finish

Have you ever quit something? I guess we all quit at one time or another. I mean, quitting isn't all that hard. Nehemiah 6:15 says, "So the wall was completed on the twenty-fifth of Elul, in fifty-two days." Now I don't know what Elul is, maybe it's like saying "September." What I do know is that Nehemiah set out to rebuild the wall in Jerusalem that had been torn down and he didn't just start the work, he completed it. The wall surrounded the whole city, so it was plenty big. Certainly others had thought about rebuilding the wall, but it was Nehemiah who started the work and finished it. Starting something is easy, and giving up on something is easy, but finishing something takes effort. Sometimes I can't even finish a puzzle. While a puzzle doesn't play an integral role in my destiny, there are other things in life that are important. What can you finish? Well, with God's help you can finish anything. Nehemiah was surrounded by people who told him this work couldn't be done. He was surrounded by people who opposed what he was doing, but Nehemiah wouldn't give up. He persevered. Perseverance is continuing on even when it seems pointless and even when it seems like a better idea to quit. Perseverance quite often seems to defy logic and can seem quite reckless. But perseverance is what we need if we want to finish.

Truth You Can Believe In

Sometimes I hear stories and I wonder if they're true. I mean, should I believe everything I hear? Like the news or a movie that is based on a true story—I wonder, *Is this really true or does it just have a bit of truth in it?* Sometimes I wonder if what I'm hearing is just a big pack of lies. Isaiah 53:1 says, "Who has believed our message and to whom has the arm of the LORD been revealed?" The only real truth left—truth that doesn't sway with the times, public opinion, or the next Spiderman movie—is the Bible. But just because it's absolute truth, doesn't mean everyone believes it. Believing in God's Word is a choice. It's a choice to believe that the Bible really is God speaking and that it is infallible, which means there aren't any man-made mistakes accidentally in the Bible. We can't approach the Bible as though it is *based* on a true story (if you do, then you are building your life on sand). We must believe it to be the absolute truth, straight from God. So God asks, "Who believes the message? I mean *really* believes." And then He says "and to whom has the arm of the Lord been revealed?" The arm of the Lord is His strength becoming evident in your life. When you choose to believe God's Word, that is when His strength can truly become active in your life. We're talking about God's arm, and believe me when I say that He's got some guns! Have you ever needed something bigger than you, a miracle, something impossible? Well, believe in God's Word, and let God's arm come and hook you up with victory!

Eating Better

The devil likes to mess with what you eat. No, really! Think about the very first temptation. It was about food: "How about a little tasty fruit?" The devil tempted Eve with the fruit of the knowledge of good and evil. Never eat a piece of fruit that has a name that long. Sadly, Eve fell for Satan's trick. How about when the devil came and tempted Jesus? (Check out Matthew 4:1-11.) The first thing he brought up was food. He told Jesus to turn the rock into bread. But Jesus wasn't buying it. When it comes to you, the devil would love it if you wasted your body away downing Twinkies and soda. But you've got a lot of stuff to get done here on earth, so you need to take care your body. Think of it this way: You would never put a bunch of junk in your car's gas tank, and then expect it to get you where you want to go. I'm not saying we need to be all legalistic about what we put in our mouths, but what I am saying is that we should eat better. So stop shoving in whatever is convenient, fast, or tastes good. If you can control your body enough to eat right, then you can probably overcome anything!

Let's Talk About Church

Ephesians 1:22-23 says, "God placed all things under his (Jesus') feet and appointed him to be head over everything for the church, which is his body." God put Jesus is in charge of the church. This tells me that church is incredibly important to God. You may ask, "Can't I just have church at home? I mean, I want to just rest on Sundays." Maybe you don't always like everything about church. Does that mean you can just choose not to go? Well, what does Jesus have to say about it? After all, He's head of the church. Jesus says in John 15:5, "If a man remains in me and I in him, he will bear much fruit; apart from me you can do nothing." How do we remain in Christ except to be connected to His body, which is the church? Going to church provides a charge of inspiration from God's Word for our personal growth. It makes us better. Pastors can get from God a message that is specifically for their congregation. This provides an amazing advantage to those who attend church. When you attend a church, you might meet people who aren't perfect; they might even make mistakes. I wonder if that's Jesus' way of teaching you how to love unconditionally, how to serve, how to forgive, and how not to be judgmental. After all, church is meant to be a family, and who hasn't had to learn to love and accept their brothers and sisters?

Fix Our Eyes on Jesus

What are you here to do? Hebrews 12:1 says, "Let us run with perseverance the race marked out for us." Imagine a runner stepping up to the blocks—*On your marks, get set,... oh wait, where am I running?* God has a specific purpose for your existence, a race that He's marked out for you. But how do you know what that is? Where are the markers? The passage goes on to tell us how we can find the path marked out for us when it says, "Let us fix our eyes on Jesus, the author and perfecter of our faith..." (v. 2). Our purpose can be discovered when we allow Jesus to author and perfect our faith. An author writes a book. Jesus wants to write your faith story and perfect it. We keep our eyes fixed on Jesus, even though He's invisible, by reading the words He said and following His example in the way he lived. John 1 tells us that Jesus is the Word of God, so fixing your eyes on Jesus can mean studying God's Word. As you study and learn and allow the Word to author and perfect your faith—that is, what you believe—you will begin to clearly see the race that has been marked out for you. Now all you have to do is run your race with perseverance. Ready, set, go!

You Are Not an Accident

Do you ever wonder if you being here is an accident or some sort of random event? First of all, you need to know something. You are not an accident. You were destined to be here at this time, and God has a specific purpose in mind for you. Before God created the world, He planned your existence. You are not the result of chance like some sort of pull on a slot machine. Psalm 139:15-16 says, "My frame was not hidden from you when I was made in the secret place. When I was woven together in the depths of the earth, your eyes saw my unformed body. All the days ordained for me were written in your book before one of them came to be." You have been made holy and blameless as a result of the sacrifice Jesus made for us when he took all sin, past and future, to the cross. Ephesians 1:4 tells us, "For he chose us in him before the creation of the world to be holy and blameless in his sight." When God sees you, He sees righteousness. You can boldly stand before the Lord without shame. Now, what you do with the days that have been ordained for you is up to you. God has stuff for you to do. Will you step up to do it?

God's Purpose

Jonah ran from God's purpose for his life, and in so doing, ran into a lot of trouble. He got himself and those he was traveling with in a tight spot. A storm blew up on the boat he was on, and it nearly drowned all who were around him. The crew tossed him overboard, and then he was swallowed by a big fish. And you thought your day was tough! If life is crashing down all around you and you find yourself pulling others down with you, or if you feel like you've been swallowed up by this world, it may be that you have strayed away from God's path for you or maybe you're outright running from what God is calling you to do. God loves you and wants what is best for you. He wants to clothe you better than King Solomon and bless you like He did Abraham. Our God is a good and just God. But when we leave God's will we will see, like Jonah did, that life can really blow up like a storm all around us. In the end, Jonah was saved when he cried out to God. We do the straying, but God does the saving. Where are you today? Ask God about His will for your life. Say "What would You have me do? Here I am Lord, send me!"

So What Are You Waiting For?

A lot of people are *planning* on getting their life together and really making a decision for Christ and a new lifestyle, but they haven't gotten around to it just yet. Why is that? Somewhere along the line, the world has adopted the idea that a Christian life is boring and stuffy. Not mine. In a world of reaping and sowing, a Christian life is way more fun and fulfilling than anything the world has to offer. Why? Because sowing goodness reaps goodness. A cheap thrill in the world just doesn't last long enough and it's not nearly as satisfying as you thought it might be. The world's joy lasts for a moment and must always be topped. It's like when you finally got that car you'd always wanted, the one you thought would make you happy. It did, but only for a little while. Then you found that you were off pursing the next great thing. Don't get me wrong, God wants to bless you. He wants you to have nice things. But it's a mistake to try to draw your happiness from things. Draw your happiness from serving God. God's joy is complete. Don't wait to give yourself to God. There's no better time than right now to say to God, "Okay Lord, here is the rest of my life. Use me however You see fit."

Sowing and Reaping

I'm sure you've heard it said, "You reap what you sow." So, let's talk about sowing and reaping, seedtime and harvest. Genesis 8:22 says, "As long as the earth endures, seedtime and harvest, cold and heat, summer and winter, day and night will never cease." A farmer will tell you that if you plant corn, you will grow corn. Well, what does this mean to you? Whatever you currently have growing in your life, there is a good chance you planted the same thing some time ago. If all your friends have betrayed you and are talking bad about you, if you honestly think back, you'll likely find a time when you did the same to someone. You're reaping what you've sown. So what are you sowing? If you want love, sow love. If you want friendship, sow friendship. If you want hate, sow hate. What you reap depends on what seeds you plant. Galatians 6:7-8 says, "A man reaps what he sows. The one who sows to please his sinful nature, from that nature will reap destruction; the one who sows to please the Spirit, from the Spirit will reap eternal life." Hmmm, that's a tough one. Would I prefer destruction or eternal life? I think I'll go with eternal life. Ask God what you can sow today that will reap a harvest you can enjoy tomorrow.

Go and Make Disciples

We start our day off wondering what we need to do today. What are we going to wear? What time do we have to leave the house? So much to think about and do, then to top it off, in Matthew 28:19, Jesus commands us to go and make disciples of all nations. *I have to make disciples of all nations, too?* Our lives are way too busy for us to stop and think about making disciples of all nations. The thought of attempting to change the world is a bit overwhelming, and might even seem impossible. Lucky for us, nothing is impossible with God. You can change your world, by starting in YOUR world. Start with the people and places you are already around. But how do you go about reaching the people in your world? Start by inviting those people to church (this means, of course, you have to have a church). Begin to pray. It's very important to pray for your family members and friends. God will make Himself just as real to those you know as He has to you. Also, don't be afraid to tell your story. Tell them how Jesus changed you. We are all concerned about our unsaved family and friends, but it's not enough just to be concerned. We've got to do something about. I'm challenging you to come up with a plan of action, and then take action. Making disciples shouldn't just be something you think about in passing, but it should be part of your daily focus.

First, Lead Yourself

If we want to lead people to Christ, we need to learn how to lead. And before we try to lead others, we must first learn to lead ourselves. Leading yourself is the preparation part of learning to become a great leader. Preparation takes time. Jesus started His ministry by not eating for 40 days. Fasting is a great tool to put you in charge. When we don't eat, we are sending a message to our body that it is not the boss. Your body has lots of different desires, but you need to show it who's in charge. Your mind likes to think about things it just shouldn't be thinking about. Once again, you must remember that you are in charge, and you can tell your mind what to think. Sometimes your emotions might tell you that you are in a bad mood and that just makes everyone around you miserable. But remember, you're the boss of your emotions. Tell your emotions to be submitted to God's Word. All of this is learning how to lead yourself. After Jesus fasted, He was tempted. But by that time, Jesus was prepared and He didn't listen to the devil. Instead, He quoted the Word. So call your body, your mind, and your emotions into your office for a meeting and tell them that you're in charge now. Now that you know how to lead yourself, you're ready to lead others.

No Difference

Society separates all of us into little groups. The world tries to separate us by color, income bracket, political beliefs, and even the way we dress. But Paul writes in Galatians 3:28, "There is neither Jew nor Greek, slave nor free, male nor female, for you are all one in Christ Jesus." Boys rule and girls drool, sure, but in Christ, neither rules nor drools. In the interest of being more Christlike, can we stop seeing different colored skin, please? This generation is the closest man has ever been to being color-blind, not seeing one race as better than another, but we still have a very long way to go. You might find yourself putting down the poor saying, "Why don't they go get a job?" or you may judge the rich saying, "They should've sold that and given money to the poor." You may think that men are better than women or vice versa. But there is neither black nor white, nor brown nor polka dotted, no distinction between people with tattoos or without tattoos or piercings, or with green hair, or homeless—we are all one in Christ. Division will keep us crippled, but unity will bring us strength. Strength will bring influence, and influence will bring change, and this whole world could use a little changing! Remember, God looks at the heart, and that's all we need to concern ourselves with also.

It's All About the Attitude

People seem to be so concerned about attitude. All you hear is, "Get rid of that bad attitude!" So, what's the big deal about attitudes? Best selling leadership author John Maxwell states that our attitudes dictate our performance. If your attitude in life is bad, then you will be bad at life. What's the source of our attitudes? Your attitude starts with your thoughts. If you're thinking about how terrible everything is, it will come out in your attitude and then eventually in your life. And then surprise, everything will become terrible. You are today where your thoughts were yesterday, and you will be tomorrow where your thoughts are leading you today. Paul instructs us in Philippians 4:8 to think about things that are true, noble, right, pure, lovely, admirable, excellent, and praiseworthy. If you are focusing on your problems, then stop. That isn't on the list. If you are spending time thinking about what someone said about you, stop. Once again, not on the list. Maybe you're thinking about your boss and how annoying work is, or your in-laws, or how you feel lonely. Again, not on the list. "Rejoice in the Lord always. I will say it again: Rejoice!" (Philippians 4:4). Change your attitude by expecting good things today, and watch them materialize tomorrow.

What's Your Motive?

In Deuteronomy 28, we find that God wants to bless you greatly, in every way. Let's put this together with something written in James 4:2-3. It says "You do not have, because you do not ask God." What do you need? What are your desires? Don't forget to ask God. Yes, He knows what you need, but according to this scripture, He wants you to ask. The scripture goes on to say "When you ask, you do not receive, because you ask with wrong motives, that you may spend what you get on your pleasures." See, a lot of Christians are asking God for new, bigger and better stuff, but they ask with wrong motives. The motivation behind their request is all wrong. We must learn to seek first after God's kingdom, meaning, we ask for blessings so that we can be a blessing to others and to the furthering of the gospel. Ask God for things that will help His cause. Become God-minded and offer yourself as a living sacrifice, willing to do what He wants you to do. Then you are seeking God's kingdom, and He will be faithful and just to reward you both here on earth and in heaven.

Control This

Have you ever been cruising through a great day and someone comes in and ruins it? All it takes is for someone to come along and talk bad about you or to you, whether it's your close friend or some grocery store clerk, and suddenly, you are miserable. What you need to accept is that you cannot control everything that goes on around you. Your environment has many variables in it. The only thing you have complete control of is you. So don't give people the power to make you feel bad. I can't control what people say or what people do, but I can control how I react to those things. If you find out someone is bad mouthing you, just go to them and ask, "What's up?" If you approach people in an unthreatening manner, you will be amazed what can be worked out. If you start a conversation by yelling at someone, you'll get nowhere. Control yourself and say, "Hey, this is what I heard. I don't think you're like that, but I thought you should know what's going around." In doing this, you'll make friends, not enemies. If you learn to focus on the one thing you can control—your reaction—you will find your life will begin to have far more ups than downs.

Thirsty?

In Isaiah 55, God invites all who are thirsty to come. Are you thirsty? God has just what you need so that you will thirst no more. John 4 tells of a conversation between Jesus and a Samaritan woman in which He said, "Whoever drinks the water I give him will never thirst" (v. 14). We run around trying to fulfill our desires with what the world has to offer. The problem is that you can quench your thirst with the world's ways, but it will only last a moment. You can buy moments of joy with drinking or different kinds of drugs, but it's not going to last. You need to eat and drink what Jesus has for you. His Spirit and His Word will fill you up, and instead of leaving you empty and lost, you'll be better than before. God wants to fill you up to overflowing so that you can pass on to others the joy and peace He has given you. Once you experience fulfillment with God, you'll never go back because those old things can't satisfy like He can.

Fervent Prayer

In First Samuel 1, there was a lady named Hannah and she was having some trouble. She wanted to have a baby. Yes, she was married, but the Word says that the Lord had closed her womb. So Hannah prayed for a son—a lot. The Bible says she wept bitterly as she cried out to the Lord. A lot of Christians will say that God has given them a thorn, something that they don't like to live with but they have decided it is from God. Well, I encourage them to do what Hannah did. She didn't accept her circumstances. She didn't just say "Oh, this is God's will for my life so I'll just live like this." Hannah prayed fervently. You may have lived your whole life with something like allergies or a handicap, but don't accept it anymore. Pray like Hannah did, because Hannah was indeed given a son. In fact, she was given six children. God is good and His love endures. He made good on His promise to give us His son and He will make good on the promises to send His blessings into our lives. Pray fervently to the Lord. Then believe that He has heard and answered your prayers, and you will have the perfect will of the Lord.

It's Not that Complicated

The other day, a guy told me that Jesus wasn't God. He could not be more incorrect and I can prove it to you in about one minute. John 1 says the Word was with God, and the Word was God, and the Word became flesh and dwelt among us. Now Jesus is the one who became flesh and dwelt among us. When this passage talks about the Word, it is referring to Jesus, who was with God, and was God, and became flesh and dwelt among us. There are those who will tell you that Jesus should not be worshipped because He is not God, but was only a man who was a great teacher. However, both Matthew 1 and Isaiah 7 refer to Jesus as *Immanuel*, which means "God with us." You see, sometimes people try and over complicate the Bible, but the Bible isn't complicated. Psalm 49:7 says that "No man can redeem the life of another." Yet, Jesus redeemed us from sin. So… if Jesus were only a man, and not God, then it would not have been possible for Him to redeem us from sin. The truth is that Jesus is God and He took on the flesh of a man to make redemption available to us all through His work and our faith in Him. God wishes that every knee would bow and every tongue confess that Jesus Christ is Lord. Not man, but Lord!

Insight

Get up, go to school, do your homework and study, go to bed; get up, go to school, do your homework and study, go to bed and don't forget about preparing for college! The importance of knowledge is revealed in our daily routine. It seems that a great deal of our time is spent trying to accumulate knowledge. But understanding is better than knowledge. Adam and Eve knew the fruit was forbidden, but that knowledge wasn't enough to keep them safe. If life has a test in it, I may know the answer, but if I have no understanding to properly apply the answer, I will fail the test. Psalm 119:99 says "I have more insight than all my teachers, for I meditate on your statutes." Here, the word "statutes" is referring to the Word of God. God's Word has all of the real answers in it. By spending time thinking about His Word, pondering it, asking Him about it, and reading it, you will gain insight. Insight is more than knowing; it's understanding. If you have insight, when everyone else around you is following whatever new trend is going on and going in the wrong direction, you will be able to step around the crowd and stay on the high ground of life. No longer will you be spending life living from problem to problem, but instead you will find yourself living blessing to blessing. So, in all of your studies, make sure you include the most important study—focusing on God's Word—that you may gain what is truly best.

The Sum of It All

'It seems like there are so many rules to remember when you're a Christian. It reminds me of how I've felt about swinging a golf club—*with so many things to remember, I'll probably forget to hit the ball.* But Jesus broke it down for us so we'd understand the essence of being a Christian. He said in Matthew 22:37-40 "'Love the Lord your God with all your heart and with all your soul and with all your mind.' This is the first and greatest commandment. And the second is like it: 'Love your neighbor as yourself.' All the Law and the Prophets hang on these two commandments." The book of Romans tells us that love is the fulfillment of the law. So all the rules we find in the Old Testament, all of the lessons, traditions, symbols, prophecies, and whatever else added up, comes down to this: love God, love others. Just two things to remember. But it all hinges on understanding God's kind of love. For instance, God's love is not selfish. So if you find yourself trying to take advantage of your girlfriend, then you don't love her. You missed it. Once you begin to understand God's love, you put yourself in a position to love God's way. And that, according to Jesus, is the most important thing.

Choose Wisely

Who are your friends? I mean really, with whom do you surround yourself? You've heard it said, "You will become who you hang around." We should carefully handpick our friends. Pick someone who will make you better. You might be saying, "Yeah, but Jesus hung out with the sinners." Those closest to Jesus were His disciples, whom He handpicked. He chose them! So how do we know what to look for in a friend? In John 21, Jesus appeared to the disciples but only John recognized that it was Jesus. He leaned over to his friend Peter, pointed and said, "It is the Lord." Now this is the kind of friend you want in your life. You want a friend who points you to Jesus! I mean, the world has enough bad influence in it, so why would we want friends who influence us to do wrong as well? The Bible tells us "Bad company corrupts good character" (1 Corinthians 15:33). We are just setting ourselves up to fail when we hang around the wrong kind of friends. If Jesus was choosy about His friends while here on earth, shouldn't we be, also?

Bitter Roots

Ever have someone hurt you or hurt one of your friends? Hebrews 12:15 says, "See to it that… no bitter root grows up to cause trouble and defile many." When someone hurts you or someone you know, a bitter root can start growing. Your anger, judgment, or unforgiveness of a person actually ends up hurting you. You may act out of hurt in order to get back at someone—that's called revenge—but in the end, the one hurt by those acts is you. If someone "*makes* you feel" a certain way, don't you see you have given that person control over how you feel?! Don't let people control how you feel! Jesus said to pray for those who persecute you and to forgive. It's easy to be mad and talk bad about others, but that only leads to trouble. So be big enough to forgive when you don't want to, and pray for the other person so that you remain accountable for your own life. Now don't get me wrong. I'm not saying that you shouldn't defend yourself or others during an attack, that's different. I'm talking about forgiving others after the incident and not looking to get revenge. Vengeance is the Lord's because He's the one best equipped to handle it.

Love Discipline?

Does it make you angry when you get in trouble? How about when your boss is breathing down your neck about something? Do you find yourself saying stuff under your breath because you are mad? Proverbs 12:1 says, "Whoever loves discipline loves knowledge, but he who hates correction is stupid." Now, the word *stupid* here is a pretty strong term. It's not very politically correct. Nobody wants to be stupid, but I guess sometimes we act stupid. It's easy to get angry when we get in trouble—angry that we got caught, or angry because someone we know is doing something we perceive as worse, or angry because we think we know more than everyone else. Anger comes easily to us, but it produces nothing. It's much harder to be disciplined and say to yourself, "Well, this correction is good. I need this. I really learned something today." That seems impossible, but it's what God wants from us. If we want to be godly, like Christ, we have to change. Change comes when we realize that the way we've been doing things is wrong. Sometimes that realization comes when we get in trouble and are corrected, so maybe getting in trouble isn't always bad. The next time you're in trouble, try a different approach. Attempt to love discipline. It's actually the smart thing to do!

Speak Life

Have you ever had something happen to you that you refuse to talk about or think about, yet somehow the hidden memories try to control you? Serious events can leave scars and dead areas in our life. They can make us incapable of truly trusting or loving, or they can work to keep us in depression. In Ezekiel 37, the prophet Ezekiel had a vision of dead bones in a valley and the Lord told him to speak life into those bones using God's words. When the prophet spoke the words, the bones became flesh and blood. They went from death to life. God wants this to happen to the dead areas in your life. The key is to speak life into those areas. Don't relive the past. Forgive and move on. Speak life and joy into your dead bones. The Word of God is life, and it brings life, so speak God's Word. Be positive and with the power of God's Word, bring life to every area of your existence.

Stay On God's Path

When I'm driving by myself, I always get lost. I always miss my turn, which means I have to make U-turns or pull into a parking lot to turn around. It makes every trip take longer and it's frustrating. In John 16:1, Jesus states "All this I have told you so that you will not go astray." The instructions He has given us in the Bible are there so that we won't miss our turns. If you go through life trying to navigate using the advice of your friends or your own past experiences, you will have many U-turns to make. God's Word is the map we need. It has the direction we need. The answers are all there. It even tells you the various speed limits of life so you won't find yourself going too fast—or too slow. So, get your Bible out. God wants you on His path where there is safety, adventure and no U-turns are required.

Keep the Flies Out

Ecclesiastes 10:1 says, "As dead flies give perfume a bad smell, so a little folly outweighs wisdom and honor." What do you get out of this scripture? Does it mean you should never leave your perfume bottle open in a room full of flies that are dying? I think as a general rule, you shouldn't allow any kind of dead thing near your perfume bottle. That stuff is expensive. It's best to leave the cap on and do your best to keep insects out of the bottle. I think the scripture is saying that your life may smell like perfume right now, but there are friends and things you can get involved with that are like dead flies. If you allow them to do so, they will infiltrate your sweet smelling life and turn it rancid. God wants your life to be a sweet fragrance to Him, so be careful who you hang out with and what you allow to influence your life. Don't be afraid to break up with a friend or an activity that stinks. Smell good, bathe often in the truth of God's Word, and keep the flies out.

Scalps or Scallops?

My son Christian's birthday was coming up and he asked me if there were any holidays or special events that fell on the same day as his birthday. So I jumped online and found out that his birthday is the same day as Baked Scallops Day. Now Christian didn't find that funny, but I did. So nearly every day when I saw him I'd say, "Hey, can't wait til Baked Scallops Day? Eh?" One day he said, "Dad, that doesn't even make sense. Why would anyone take off the top of someone's head and bake it?" I said, "It's not 'scalps,' it's 'scallops'—it's a type of fish." Sometimes we misunderstand the Word of God because we misunderstand His terms. When God talks to us in His Word about love, we may have a different definition in our mind of what kind of love He's talking about. We have to learn what God means in His Word when He talks about prosperity, health, love, joy, peace, or whatever you are learning about. When I want to learn what God has to say about a particular topic, I look up every scripture in the Bible that contains words describing the topic, and then I study them. I ask the Holy Spirit to lead me to truth, and then I listen. Allow God's Word to re-define how you think, then there will be no more misunderstandings.

Eden

In Genesis 1, in the beginning, God and Adam were hanging out in the Garden of Eden. God created this beautiful world and the greatest place in all the world—the garden of Eden—He reserved as a home for man. This place had more than the man needed. It would be like staying at a ritzy hotel, and when you were checking in, you found out that God had already paid for you to stay in the Presidential Suite. God created the very best for you. "Well I thought that God wants me to suffer." No! That's not right. He wants the best for you, but He doesn't want you to make things your focus. See, that was what was so awesome about the Garden of Eden: It was a place where God could come and hang out with Adam every day. God wanted Adam to put their relationship first and He wants the same thing from us. He wants us to talk with Him in prayer, to approach Him with boldness through the blood of Jesus. Spend some time with Him every day, reading His words or singing Him a song. If you make your relationship with God your number one priority, then wherever you are, it's Eden for you.

Where's Your Delight?

The grass often does seem greener on the other side of the fence. Psalm 37:1 says, "Do not…be envious of those who do wrong." Why would we ever be envious of those who do wrong? Well, because the people who do wrong things appear to be having fun. "YEEEAH! Hey, look at me! I'm so drunk, I can hardly put together a complete sentence! Woohoo!" Those people might even try to make you feel left out because you aren't joining in. Don't be envious of those people. Stop thinking that you are missing out. The Bible goes on to say "Like the grass they will soon wither, like green plants they will soon die away… Delight yourself in the LORD and He will give you the desires of your heart" (vv. 2,4). Delight yourself in doing wrong and you'll wither. Delight yourself in God and His ways, and you will have your deepest heart's desires. Now who's envious?

Fear

Jesus was out walking on the water – that may not surprise you any-more, but it freaked out the disciples. They got scared. So Jesus said, "Take courage! It is I. Don't be afraid" (Matthew 14:27). There are a lot of things a person could be afraid of. What Jesus was saying to His disciples and what He's saying to us is "Don't be afraid." Back to our story—when Peter saw Jesus, he stepped out into the water and tried walking on it. When he realized that people don't naturally walk on water, he got scared and began to sink. But Jesus caught him. Jesus will do the same thing for us when we are sinking, but Jesus' goal is for us to have no fear of this world. He wants us to trust in Him with all of our heart, and lean not on our own understanding. Our understanding is that people sink in water. We know that with God, all things are possible, but fear can crowd out that knowledge. We can stop fear by taking our thoughts captive. So if fear is coming at you to take control of your mind and say with confidence, "(The Lord) is my refuge and my fortress, my God, in whom I trust" (Psalm 91:2).

Just One Lie

Genesis 3 tells us that the serpent was more crafty than any of the wild animals. That's right, the devil is sneaky. He talked Eve into eating the fruit that they were told not to eat. The devil convinced her saying, "You will not surely die…For God knows that when you eat of it, your eyes will be opened, and you will be like God, knowing good and evil" (Genesis 3:4). First of all, if a snake ever starts talking to you, don't listen. The serpent was taking God's truth and making it into a lie. To win, the devil just needed Eve to believe one lie: "You can be like God." That's what makes the devil so sneaky. He just needs to get you to believe one lie. He wants you to think it's okay to get just a little drunk. Or he might tell you, "Hey, the Bible doesn't say not to get high." Or he might try and convince you your husband doesn't love you anymore so it's OK to get emotionally involved with that nice guy. Eve believed the lie, ate the fruit, gave some to Adam, and it cost mankind 4000 years of bondage. When temptation comes, ask yourself, "Is that crafty devil trying to trap me?" Without a doubt, the answer is ***yes***.

Lessons from the Blind Men

In Matthew 10, two blind men kept following Jesus around asking for mercy. They wanted to see. So Jesus asked them, "Do you believe that I am able to do this?" "Yes Lord," they replied. Then Jesus touched their eyes and healed them. There are areas in your life, both spiritual and physical, that might be in need of a little healing. We can learn a lot from the story of the two blind men. First, they had to ask for healing. If you need healing, ask for it. Next, realize that Jesus is asking you a question—"Do you believe that I am able to do this?" Well do you? Remember that Jesus could perform very few healings in His own hometown because the people there did not believe. Unbelief will keep you sick and in need. So ask Jesus for your healing and believe that He is able to heal you. The same God of miracles in the Bible is our great God today. Remember, as crowds of people came to Jesus for healing, Jesus never once said *NO*.

Don't Be a Stiff Kneecap

Ninety percent of Americans claim to be Christians, but only about fourteen percent go to church weekly. Hmmm... Not that church is the be-all-end-all to being a Christian, but why do so many who claim to be Christ followers not go? Many say, "I got burned at church." Then they recount some great sob story that is horrifying to everyone. Rather than drop out, here's a different approach to consider. If you have values that the church needs, then bring them to the church. Help change what it is that hurt you. Help the church become more relevant and authentic. The church is the body of Christ, which says to me that it must be important. You see Christ needs to get some stuff done in the world. He does that through the church and as long as you refuse to be a part of the body that gets that stuff done, you're just like a kneecap that won't bend on the body of Christ. See, church isn't for you and what you can get; it's for others and what you can give them. The church isn't supposed to reach inward, it reaches outward. So you got burned at church once. I got burned cooking waffles the other day. I'll still cook waffles. I'll just wear mitts. So get your mitts on, go to church and cook some waffles.

Steal, Kill and Destroy

Jesus said in John 10:10, "The thief comes only to steal, kill, and destroy; I have come that they may have life, and have it to the full." There is a very real enemy that, for today, we will refer to as the devil. Now if the devil's main job is to steal, kill, and destroy, then this is someone you want far away from your life. But how do we get rid of him? In James 4:7, the Word teaches us to "Submit yourselves, then, to God. Resist the devil, and he will flee from you." Resist him, and he will flee. That's it? Seems simple enough, huh? When the little voice from the wrong shoulder tells you to do things that you know you shouldn't be doing, resistance will send that voice packing. Learn how to say "*Noooo*, I'm not listening to you today." Resistance starts with refusing to listen. If you listen to the devil, you give him permission to mess with your life. Resist the devil's attempts to steal, kill and destroy and you'll be well on your way to the abundant life Jesus promises.

What Do You Say About Yourself?

What kinds of things do you say about yourself? How do you describe yourself to others? In Matthew 16, Jesus changed Simon's name to Peter. Simon means "reed," but Peter means "rock." You see, Jesus knew someone would need to be a leader after His work here was done and He returned to heaven, but Peter wasn't quite ready. He needed to become a rock. Remember, Peter was the guy who denied that he even knew Jesus three times, and then he completely bailed on his friend while He was crucified. All of Peter's life, he had referred to himself as "reed," and so did others. Jesus needed Peter to begin to see himself differently, so that he could become all that God wanted him to be. We need to begin to see ourselves differently. We sometimes say, "I'm not that smart," or "I am not very talented," or "I have a handicap," or "I get sick easily," or "I'm not pretty because I have a big nose." We may think this is being humble, but Jesus was humble, and I don't ever remember Him saying anything like that about Himself. Jesus was incredibly confident in the way God created Him, which in fact is a compliment to the Creator. So change what you say about yourself. Then others will begin to speak differently about you, and you will have taken another step towards the success that God has for you.

Dating—Part One

There are so many opinions about dating and a million books have been written about it. So what does the Bible have to say about dating? A lot of people start talking about guarding your heart, which is instruction that can be found in Proverbs 4:23, but that instruction actually has nothing to do with dating. It has to do with what words we hear. So back to dating – in Genesis 28, we find a story of a wonderful romance done God's way. The chapter opens with Jacob going off to find a wife. This is key all by itself. Most people are dating, regardless of the season they are at in their life. Jacob, however, didn't just date; he went looking for a wife because he was at a stage in his life when he was ready to be married. That is God's plan. Too often, people end up dating seriously too young, lives change and move on, and people have their hearts broken. God never intends for hearts to be broken. In fact, Jesus came to heal the broken hearted. God has a much better plan for dating. When you are ready to be married, God will bring you the one He has for you. So before you are ready, take care of yourself. Don't run around becoming emotionally or physically involved with a bunch of people you were never intended to end up with. Save yourself for the one God has for you, knowing that He will only bring you the best.

Dating—Part Two

Let's talk about dating some more. Another thing we can take from Jacob's story in Genesis 28 is that he went to the place his parents instructed him to go to find a wife. Jacob's mom told him, "Please don't marry a Canaanite woman." Your mom might be saying, "Please don't marry some guy you met online!" Here's my point: God has given special insight to your parents about Mr. or Mrs. Right, so pay attention. If Mom or Dad is saying, *No way!* about someone you met, then you may want to listen up. Don't assume your parents have been placed in your life to serve as a killjoy. In reality, God may be speaking through them to save you from trouble and heartbreak.

Dating—Part Three

Okay, I know this is three days in a row on dating, but I had to do another one! Perhaps the most important lesson we learn from Jacob's story in Genesis 28 is that he didn't go looking for Mrs. Right until he was ready to be married. Looking for a mate before you are ready to be married is like buying ice cream, but not owning a freezer. It's just going to end in a mess. If you go looking for a mate before you're ready, chances are good you'll end up falling in love with the wrong person and that always turns out badly for everyone involved. You see, Jacob fell in love with Rachel, his future wife, in less than 30 days. It happened quickly. Now, they didn't get married for some time, but they were in love. Jacob gave his heart to Rachel, risking everything, putting it all on the line for love. He could do that because he was ready. Don't ever think of doing this while still in high school because you have other things you should be focused on at this time in your life, like homework! However, when you are ready for marriage, give it your all. Give your marriage the kind of start that people will want to hear about for years to come.

Dream Big

I find that so many people give up on their dreams because someone in their life has thought it was necessary to "give them a reality check." Dreams seem impossible, but that's what makes them so fun to chase. We need to understand that with God *all* things are possible. God wants you to reach so high that the only way you can attain your goal is with His help. If we can do everything on our own, then we may begin to foolishly believe that we don't need God. That's no good. God wants to work in your life to show you that He is strong where you are weak. When Nehemiah went chasing after his dream to rebuild the city wall in Jerusalem, he was met with discouragement from many who should have been supportive. Sometimes those closest to us don't understand where we are going. But Nehemiah said, "The God of heaven will give us success" (Nehemiah 2:20). The God of heaven will give you success as well. So, step out into the land of superheroes and watch the God of heaven get all the glory. And if you fall down, or your cape gets twisted around you, well, try again. You only truly fail when you quit. If you haven't quit yet, then you haven't lost; you were just learning something new that you will need on your journey.

Trust God

In Daniel 6, we see the protagonist, Daniel, tossed into the lion's den to be eaten. Now Daniel could've reacted to this by saying "Well, I guess it's just my time to go. God must have decided to take me. Come on lions, dinner's ready." This is the reaction we often have when we are put in a situation where it looks like all is lost and there is no hope. But instead of giving in to certain death, Daniel trusted God. Daniel 6:23 says, "no wound was found on him, because he had trusted in his God." It doesn't say no wound was found because God rescued him, it instead points out that it was Daniel's trust that put him in a position where God could save him. Psalm 143:8 says, "Let the morning bring me word of your unfailing love, for I have put my trust in you." God's love never fails, but you have a responsibility to put your trust in the Lord. Sometimes it's hard to trust when everyone and everything in your life is headed towards defeat. But God says to trust Him. Don't trust only in what you can understand. Trust God and watch the impossible become possible in your life.

Wherever You Are, Be You

Who are you? Whoever you are, however you talk, whatever kinds of things you do, be that person all the time. At school, the job, church, home, wherever you are you should just be you. If there is something you need to change about yourself, then make that change no matter where you are. Jesus said in Luke 8:17 that there is nothing concealed that will not be made known. The parts of our lives that we try to hide will be revealed anyway, so don't hide things. Jesus said that we are the light of the world, and we need to put that light on a stand for all to see. We should be strong enough and have enough integrity inside of us to be the same person no matter who we are around. Don't act to impress, and don't conform to your surroundings. Don't be concerned with what people think, instead care about what God sees in you. Remember, God is with you no matter where you go and He knows the intent of your heart. He wants to see you win in all areas of your life!

How God Sees You

Sometimes we don't think very highly of ourselves. But I want you to know how God sees you. In Matthew 11:11 Jesus said, "Among those born of women there has not risen anyone greater than John the Baptist; yet he who is least in the kingdom of heaven is greater than he." Of all of those born up to the point of Jesus, none is seen as greater than the very least in the kingdom of heaven. When you receive Jesus, you receive access to the kingdom of heaven. You could be the "least in the kingdom," a very weak Christian, and yet God still sees you as great. You have to begin to see yourself the way God sees you. He sees you as mighty and strong; He sees you as holy and blameless. Really. He has something huge for you to do for Him, and He needs you! That's right, God needs you the same way He needed David to stand up for what's right. Just like He needed Nehemiah to accept his role in rebuilding the wall, God needs you. Your job then is to begin to see yourself as God sees you so that you can step into your destiny and begin to do what He has asked.

The Cure for Loneliness

Do you ever feel alone? I mean really alone. No matter how much money you have, no matter your social status, you can be alone. Whether you have two loving parents or no parents, loneliness doesn't care about these kinds of things. You can be surrounded by people and still feel alone. There are lots of songs about being lonely. I Googled it and found 52 different songs about loneliness, but I don't think singing about or listening to songs about loneliness will help you cope. Well, there is good news for the lonely. Jehovah Shammah is one of the names of God, and that name means The Lord God Ever Present. So remember that wherever you go, God is there. Deuteronomy 31:6 says "He will never leave you." That's right. Right in the middle of tragedy, God is there to give you comfort and when trouble comes, Jesus is in the boat with you waiting for you to call on Him to help you through. When you get mad at someone, God is there to help you forgive, and when you feel all out of love, God has some more love for you. So even when you call around and no one is answering their phone, and you're thinking, *Well, I'm alone, who can I talk to*, you can talk to God. In fact, you could stop listening to me right now and talk to God. He's got something really cool He wants to say to you, I'll bet. And since He's God, what He has to say is probably a lot better than what I'm saying.

Where's Your Heart?

Where's your treasure? I mean where do you put your dough? When I got my first car, every penny I had went into that car. One day, my nice new paint job got a scratch from one end of the car to the other. I was so mad. Who would do such a terrible thing? It did more than mess up my week. But in the grand scheme of eternity, that car doesn't get to spend forever with me. When I started dating the girl I married, every penny I had went into gifts for her, dates, and dinner. Hey, girls are expensive, but she has my heart. Matthew 6:21 says, "For where your treasure is, there your heart will be also." So here's the question, where do I want my heart? Well I want my heart in the kingdom of God. So how do I get my heart there? Jesus made it clear. He said I need to put my treasure into the kingdom of God, and my heart will come along for the ride. Jesus has made His home in my heart, now I want to put my heart into His home, His kingdom. Remember, your car ain't going into eternity with you. Now a dude needs a car to get around and do some work, but your car doesn't need your heart, it just needs gas. God wants your heart, so pony up some dough. You may be saying, "Oh, all God wants is my money…" But that's not true, He wants your heart.

Keeping the Faith

Let me talk for just a minute about marriage. You might be saying, "I'm not married." That's okay, this is going to be good advice for anyone. Marriage is quite often mistaken as a big event, with fancy clothes, rings, and some vows. But neither vows nor rings nor fancy clothes hold a marriage together. The US census claims that 50% of all marriages end in divorce within the first 15 years. Wow—that's a lot. Now, I don't think anyone is planning to get divorced when it is their wedding day. But two people can drift apart over time. Here's the thing—marriage isn't a commitment, it is a covenant. Well, we have a covenant with God as well. So how does the covenant thing work? God has asked us to keep our covenant with Him, and we keep our covenant with God by faith. We do this by believing God is the only God, and Jesus is the only Son of God who died for us. Our covenant isn't kept by being good enough, it's kept by faith. Apply that to your marriage. You keep your covenant by having faith in your spouse, that they are the best person for you in every way. This isn't something you can do once on your wedding day. You have to keep this faith daily.

Forgiveness

Have you ever done something wrong and asked God to forgive you for it? You move on, but soon you find yourself asking God to forgive you again. Maybe a few days later, you're asking God to forgive you again for the same thing. It's like you're not sure if God has forgiven you yet. Romans 4:8 says, "Blessed is the man whose sin the Lord will never count against him." When you receive Jesus Christ, believing in your heart in what He did, and confessing with your mouth that Jesus is Lord, you gain access to redemption from sin. This means that when you ask the Lord to forgive you of sins, He does! The sin is washed away in the blood of Jesus, and you are pure. Forgiveness is not something you have to earn by beating yourself up, but forgiveness is a gift from God. So why do you keep asking God to forgive you? Well, it's because you are having a difficult time forgiving yourself. You need to learn to forgive the way God forgives! He no longer holds your sin against you, so you need to no longer hold it against yourself. Forgive yourself, or your friend, or the dog for messing up the carpet—just forgive!

Remember What You Were

So you're a Christian right? That means you're perfect in every way, right? You never have a bad desire or never do anything wrong. Well, if you're anything like me, you are still struggling through this crazy world trying to do what's right. Sometimes you win, sometimes you lose. Now, God wants us to win and has given us what we need to win, but we sometimes make wrong choices. Paul says in Titus 3:3, "At one time we too were foolish, disobedient, deceived, and enslaved by all kinds of passions and pleasures." Paul was reminding Titus and all of us to remember how much we've been forgiven, that we have left some messes behind us, and that we'll create some messes in the future, too. It's our common experiences that will draw the lost to us, our ability to relate to those who are stuck in a bind or making a bad choice. When instead of judging them or looking down on them, pretending we're always perfect, we remember that we all stumble and that any hope we've found, we've found in Jesus Christ and what He provided for us, we open the door so we can share the hope of Jesus with those in need.

Who's the Boss?

Your body has some physical desires, right? We all have the desire to eat, to sleep, and eventually, to procreate. These are all God given desires to help us. If you didn't have the desire to eat, then you might not eat and you would die of starvation. The desire to sleep is there to keep you well rested so your body doesn't break down. But the same desire that is there to help us can malfunction and end up hurting us. You could sleep all day and be lazy. Or you could eat all the wrong stuff and get sick. Athletes (and those preparing for swimsuit season) pay attention to what they eat and they exercise and get their beauty sleep. They know it's important to tame those natural desires so they benefit, not harm, the body. In I Corinthians 9:26, Paul says; "Therefore I do not run like a man running aimlessly; I do not fight like a man beating the air. No, I beat my body and make it my slave." Now Paul isn't talking about abusing his body, but he's letting his body know that he is the boss. Your spirit must be in control of your body, so don't buy into the lie your body will tell you that it needs all that chocolate cake and fast food, and that it needs to sleep until noon. Those are the things your body wants to do, not what it needs. Take charge of your physical desires so that you can run your race for the Lord without interruption!

The Power of Words

The Bible talks again and again to us about the power of our words. Proverbs 18:21 tells us, "The tongue has the power of life and death, and those who love it will eat its fruit." When John the Baptist's dad, Zechariah, began to speak in disbelief, doubting the message that his wife was going to give birth to John, the angel of the Lord made it so he couldn't speak until the child was born. Your words are powerful in your life. Are you speaking positive things or negative? In an experiment in Japan, they found that when water is being frozen, if you speak negative words to the water then the molecules freeze in a chaotic pattern. But if you speak of love and happiness, the water molecules freeze in beautiful and orderly patterns. At a school in China, the students had two containers of rice and every day they would say to the one container "you fool" and to the other container they would say "thank you." The rice in the "you fool" container turned black while the other container of "well thanked" rice stayed fresh. At my church, we wrote negative words on a piece of paper and taped them on one apple. Then we wrote positive words on a piece of paper and taped them on another apple. The apple with positive words stayed fresh for seven weeks, but the one with negative words was rotten by the fourth week. Try an experiment of your own, but not just on fruit. Be positive with yourself and others and watch the results.

Distractions

Have you ever tried doing something and you were really into it, but then you kept getting interrupted? It's like when you've made yourself a really great meal and you've just sat down at the table to eat, and then someone rings the doorbell. Frustrating, huh? Well, that is exactly what sin does to us. It distracts us. Now sin can make a mess of a lot of stuff, but one of the worst things it does is distract us from what we should be doing. Too many of us have been distracted by sin so we're not doing what God needs for us to do. When David heard Goliath was blaspheming God, he saw the need for someone to fight Goliath, he acted on it, and we are still talking about it today. Every day you encounter needs in this world, needs other people have that God intends for you to meet. We can't afford to be distracted by sin— we need to be doing positive things here on earth. Hebrews 12:1 says, "…let us throw off everything that hinders and the sin that so easily entangles…" You know what distractions take you off course. I'll bet you're thinking about them right now! Throw them off and begin to add life and light to everyone you meet!

Big Desires

What are your deepest desires? Desires that stir inside of us drive us to do a lot of the things we do. Advertisers recognize this power, and so they show us food that looks good or the car that everyone can't help but want. They know stirring up desire works. All too often, we allow random input to stir our desires and then we go all different directions. But, a righteous man's steps are ordered of the Lord. God has a very specific road for us to follow. Colossians 3:2 says, "Set your minds on things above, not on earthly things." God wants us to set our desires on things that are higher, to reach for the stars, to dream big. God wants to give you the deep desires of your heart that will point you to your destiny. All too often, we set our desires on low things. You want that chicken meal you saw on TV, but anyone can buy a chicken meal. God wants you to set your desire on something that you will need His help to accomplish. Let God direct you to big desires so that with His help, you can do big things in your life.

Grace

Galatians 2:21 says, "I do not set aside the grace of God, for if righteousness could be gained through the law, Christ died for nothing!" Notice that our goal is to attain righteousness. Righteousness means that when God looks at your life, He's thinking, *Yeah, you're holy, blameless, and perfect.* You may be thinking, *That's not me, I don't obey all the rules.* Well, I have a great answer for that. Righteousness has nothing to do with the rules. The Scripture says that righteousness cannot be gained through the law, which is the rules. Most people are thinking that they can't talk to God because of the mistakes they have made. They distance themselves from God, or they think that God won't answer their prayers because they aren't good enough. God said He would never leave you nor forsake you. Never!! We are all trying to be good enough, but we can't possibly obey all the rules. God knows that about us, so He says if we will just believe in Jesus and what He did, then ask God to forgive us for the times we mess up, He will forgive us and even forget about it. Does that mean you should just have a big sin fest? Of course not! We are to live our lives with integrity and character because we are in debt to what Jesus did for us when He died for our sin. The key is to let the grace of God teach us to live better.

Getting to Give

How nice is your car? Mine is really nice. Is that okay? First John 3:17 says, "If anyone has material possessions and sees his brother in need but has no pity on him, how can the love of God be in him?" The key to this whole passage is *love*. God is love and He is working in us to make us more like Him. It's funny how sometimes we can have plenty, but we look at someone who has even more and we think we have nothing. Comparing with others can really mess us up. The question isn't do we have enough, but do we have more than we need? The Bible tells us that God will bless us with more than we can contain. The reason He gives more than we can contain is because we need to give the overflow away. It is meant for others in need. Notice this verse from 1 John starts with, "If anyone has material possessions…" You see, having enough puts us in a position to give, which helps us show that the love of God is in us. God wants you to be blessed so that you can give, showing His love. The promises of God are there for us so that we might become a blessing. They should not lead to greed or buying a bunch of stuff we don't need, stuff we can't take with us and stuff that rots. Instead be a blessing! As you give, it will be given back to you—pressed down, shaken together, and running over. Then you will have even more to give away!

Don't Give Up!

When I was in high school, I worked at Dunkin' Donuts. (Hey, don't mock. I got free donuts.) One of my jobs there was cleaning the bathroom. That was a dirty job. The first time I cleaned the bathroom, I really got in there and scrubbed it down, got her shiny and smelling good. But I found that every day, it would get messy again. OK, can people remember to flush? After awhile, this made me want to not clean the bathroom. I was getting tired of doing a good job. Galatians 6:9 says "Let us not become weary in doing good, for at the proper time we will reap a harvest if we do not give up." Anyone can do average work or get tired of pushing himself. Most do. But God wants us to excel in everything we do. He is telling us that if we will stay at it, not getting tired, but pushing to do a good job at everything we do, we will find ourselves beginning to excel. Most people will give up after a time. But the one who does not give up, and instead endures, pushing to be great at the most mundane and unglamorous task, the one who presses on and through will reap the harvest in the end. And a harvest that comes from God is going to be more reward than you could ever imagine. So no giving up, go get the Pine Sol!

Watch Where You Set That

Colossians 3:1 reads, "Since, then, you have been raised with Christ, set your hearts on things above." Verse two goes on to say "Set your *minds* on things above, not on earthly things." Where do you set your heart? "Well I really had my heart set on a piece of that cheesecake." Or maybe you set your heart on some boy. How about your mind? What is your mind set on? Your mind is set on whatever you spend most of your time thinking about or what you are watching or listening to and surrounding yourself with. Your heart tends to gravitate toward whatever you set your mind upon. Thoughts are seeds that are planted in your heart. If you are thinking about God's Word, you plant seeds in your heart that grow up into love and wisdom, joy and peace. If you are thinking about ice cream, you will grow in your heart the very strong urge to eat some ice cream. It's your decision where to set your heart and mind, but God tells us to set our heart and mind on things above. These are the things of God—things like helping our friends be successful, praying, reading the Word of God, finding a way to get along with our brother or honor our parents, giving, being a great wife or husband or parent or kid. Sure, these aren't always normal things to think about. But God doesn't want you to just be normal, He has made you extraordinary.

Attacks

Who's attacking you today? In Isaiah 54:15, God says to us, "If anyone does attack you, it will not be my doing; whoever attacks you will surrender to you." This scripture is referring to the covenant God has made with us through Jesus Christ. It is different from the old covenant. God is the same, but the relationship has changed. Your relationship with God is different than the relationship the people had with God before Jesus came and died for us. The covenant made through the blood of Jesus is said in Hebrews to be a "new and better covenant". Don't think, however, that just because you've entered into covenant with God, there won't be any more battles to face. Many people think that being a Christian means you never get attacked. But this verse from Isaiah makes it clear that attacks will still come. It's a crazy world and we have a real enemy. The key is the promise that God gives: Whoever attacks you will surrender to you. So even in the middle of your messy circumstances, remember that you already know the outcome. God is not the attacker and He is not the problem! God is the solution to your problems and He has promised you victory.

Crouching at the Door

My brother and I battled a lot growing up. He's older, so I think he did most of the beating and I did most of the taking it. I survived though, and we are best friends now. When we both look back, we wish we hadn't fought over such small things. I'm over it now, but he did pick on me a lot. But I'm over it… hmmm. My brother and I weren't the first siblings to fight; Cain and Abel fought too. Cain was angry with Abel one day and the Lord spoke to Cain in Genesis 4:6 warning him, "Sin is crouching at your door, it desires to have you, but you must master it." Sin desires to have you so that it can destroy you. Think of the kid who takes drugs once and ends up with Hepatitis C from a needle, or think of the drunk kid who kills someone driving, or think of the moment of passion that leaves you empty and cold. Sin wants to destroy you. When you start entertaining thoughts of sin in your mind, it's crouching at your door. God is telling us we are to master sin from the outset and we are to be in control. It's your responsibility to stop sin from entering your life. Jesus has defeated its power over you, but you must still choose not to open that door and let it into your life. Learn from Cain's mistake. Identify the enemy and keep that door shut!

Different Strokes

In John 4, Jesus spoke to a Samaritan woman. This was a big deal, since Jewish people didn't like Samaritan people. But Jesus showed us a better way. He showed us that we should love one another, regardless of our differences! The Apostle Paul teaches that in Christ, there is neither Greek nor Jew, slave nor free, but that we are all the same (Galatians 3:28). I'm white. I don't know if you could tell that from my writings, but yeah, I am one white dude. I have been all over the world to Mexico, India, Japan, Cambodia, and I have experienced a ton of different cultures, foods, dialects, languages, hair styles, skin colors, and I can tell you this: We are not all the same. Most everyone who is white is taller than me, but in many of the countries I've visited, I'm pretty tall. I've met a ton of people from all different backgrounds who are smarter than me, have a better tan, and can jump higher. We look different, talk different, run different, we are different. And yet, we all share some things in common. For instance, we all came from the same Adam and Eve. Wow. That means we're all related. Now, my brother and I are pretty different. He's way smarter than me at math, and he's better at sports. But I have better hair. No matter the differences people have, I always notice that wherever I go, people share a common desire and that is a desire to know God. Many are crying out for God, and the cry sounds the same.

A Lesson in Grace

If you read Romans 6, 7, and 8, you'll get a great lesson in grace. In the beginning, God told Adam that if he sinned, he would die. When Adam sinned, you were in him. That means you automatically were born a sinner, worthy of death. But Jesus was not born from Adam. He was born from God through the Virgin Mary. This means that Jesus was not born a sinner. Now, the punishment for sin is death, but to allow for man to live, God instructed that an innocent animal could be killed in the sinner's place to atone for his sin. While on earth, Jesus lived a sinless life. Jesus was then crucified as a criminal, though He was completely innocent. By His sacrifice, He redeemed us from sin. The penalty for all the sins of the world, both past and future, died with Him on the cross. Thankfully, death could not keep Him—He came back to life and then returned to heaven. Imagine a courtroom. The accuser looks at you and claims you must die because you have sinned. However, you believe in Jesus and what He did, so you enter a plea: "I plead the blood of Jesus. Jesus already paid the penalty of sin for me." That's all it takes. You are not guilty.

Choose God—Choose Life

Here's a question that a lot of people ask: If there is a God, then why is there so much bad in the world? Well, it all comes down to the fact that God created us with a free will. We are not robots; we can decide for ourselves. In Deuteronomy 30:19 God says, "I have set before you life and death, blessings and curses. Now choose life." God gives us the choice. Unfortunately, lots of people in this world choose the wrong thing by not choosing God. It's a multiple choice test, but the greatest part of the test is that God has already given us the right answer—"Choose life." We choose everlasting life by accepting Jesus Christ as our Savior, the only begotten Son of God who died for our sins and then rose from the dead and defeated death. You can read in the Word of the many times that God's people left Him and were enslaved, oppressed, beaten and abused. This happened, not because God left them, but because they chose curses. They chose death. You don't have to live in God's blessings if you don't want to, and some people decide not to. But I encourage you to choose life. Choose God, choose life.

Hearing for Yourself

When Samuel was just a young man, he was getting ready for bed when the Lord called him. So, what did Samuel do? He ran into Eli's room and said, "Here I am. You called me?" But Eli didn't call, God did. Samuel didn't recognize the voice of God. God accepts you just as you are and He is calling you. There comes a time in your life when you need to stop running to the Eli's in your life every time you hear the call of God. You need to learn to recognize the voice of God for yourself. God is ready to do something in your life, but what He needs is an open ear. He needs someone who will hear and say, "Speak for Your servant is listening," just like Samuel finally said. God's words become clearer when He knows that you will not just listen, but will also obey His Word. God wants you to rock this world. So get quiet before the Lord, open up the Bible, and ask Him to speak to you. Listen, then obey.

Gathering

We do lots of stuff alone. You might drive alone. I mean, the car pool lane is always empty, right? But when we want to go out on the town, that isn't something we do alone. Who has a party by themselves? I mean, a party is only a party if it's got people at it. The Bible says in Zephaniah 2:1, "Gather together, gather together." Now, I didn't just accidentally repeat those words. It really says it twice. I know you probably spend some time with God alone, right? Well if not, you should. But God is telling us here that we also need to come together. Just a few verses later, it goes on to say "seek the Lord." God wants us seeking Him in a group, too. He's saying, "Hey, get together with others and let's have a party." So if you ever get the urge to just have church at home alone, remember these encouraging words: "Gather together, gather together." It doesn't matter if you don't like the sermon at church. You won't like everything. In fact, if you agree with every sermon that you hear, then you aren't growing. God asked you to gather, so get to gathering. Maybe it's not about what you are going to get when you gather. Maybe it's about what you are going to give.

Stay with the Shepherd

Psalm 23:1 says, "The LORD is my shepherd, I shall not be in want." If God is the shepherd, that makes us sheep. Now, most of us don't know much about shepherding or being sheep. We have computers now that do all that. One thing I do know, however, is that if you are a sheep, you want a shepherd. Why? Well, because the shepherd is the person who makes sure you are taken care of. A shepherd wants you to have plenty to eat and drink – good clean water and grass to keep you healthy and strong. The shepherd makes sure you are safe and don't get eaten by wolves. So how good of a shepherd is the Lord? He's so good that when you stay close to Him and go where He tells you, then you want for nothing because you have more than you need. The key here is to listen to the Shepherd and go where He tells you. I mean, if He's trying to take you to somewhere great to get something to drink, wouldn't you want to go where He leads? Stay with the Shepherd!

Lighten Up

A messy room doesn't look messy until you turn on the light. As long as it's dark in the room, you can live in filth. Your body is the temple of God, so it's kind of like a room. Cleaning it up requires some light. Jesus said in Matthew 6:22, "The eye is the lamp of the body." What are you watching with your eyes? If your eyes are watching things that you shouldn't watch, you are affecting your whole body, keeping it in darkness. But if you would change what you are looking at, you could begin to tidy up the home inside you! Change what you watch on TV, change what websites you go to, change what movies you watch. Also, change how you see others and change how you view life. Look at things more positively. Try and find the good in everything. Doing this will be like changing the light bulb in a lamp. Maybe the bulb is old and not shining as brightly or maybe it has gone completely out. God wants to brighten up your life a bit and He gives you instruction on how to make this happen. What are you looking at and how do you see it?

When You've Been Hurt

In life, you will get mad at someone—mad at parents, mad at friends, mad at your boss, mad at a teacher, mad at the dog. But being mad at someone just makes you mad, and mad is not happy. We all want a happy life, but sometimes we lose a whole day or even a whole week being mad. So who is getting hurt? We are. We steal from ourselves when we are mad. The disciples asked Jesus how many times we should forgive someone. Jesus' response was that we should forgive seventy times seven, which is the same as saying we should forgive a lot more than you might think. Forgiveness is the greatest power you have in a situation when you have been hurt. And the sooner you forgive, the quicker you can get back to being happy. Are you waiting for the other person to say they're sorry? Well, that gives them the power again! Now, there are occasions when you may need to confront someone who has hurt you or you may even need to talk to the police to protect yourself and others from illegal actions, but no matter what, you it's important that you forgive. It's the only way to get back to the joy of the Lord.

Be a Kid Again

Young kids will believe nearly anything you tell them. You can tell them that if you find a clover with four leaves, then you hunt down a two-foot tall man dressed in green and capture him, he will lead you to his pot of gold at the end of a rainbow—and they'll believe you. Kids are great at believing things. As we get older, we get more doubtful about anything we hear; we want to see something before we believe it. But Jesus taught that to enter the Kingdom of Heaven, we must become as children. Now, He doesn't want us to reverse aging. No amount of plastic surgery can do that! Jesus was saying that we need to recapture the faith that a child has and the ability to fully believe in something that we haven't seen. Romans 10:17 teaches that faith comes by hearing the Word of God. Faith doesn't come from seeing, but hearing. Faith is evidence of things unseen. If you see it, then it isn't faith; it's knowledge. God is looking for people who will believe in Him without having to see. So open up the Bible and start being a kid again!

Learn the Lesson

Hebrews 12:7 says to "Endure hardship as discipline." Let's break this down so we can do what it says. First, "hardship" implies that sometimes life gets tough. No kidding! God is teaching us to treat hardship as though it were discipline. He didn't say it *is* discipline, He tells us to look at is *as* discipline. When a child is disciplined, the goal of the parent is to help the child grow and not repeat the mistakes that may have brought on the hardship. So this scripture is teaching us to find a way to grow a bit every time hardship comes. This means asking, "What can I learn from this?" and then taking the lesson to heart. If you don't want to learn from the hardship, then all you have to do is find a way to blame someone else for your problem. Obedience to this word means we must take some sort of responsibility to grow up and become stronger every time the winds of trouble come to make our life a bit more difficult. Either we learn to persevere and change in trials, or we destine ourselves to repeat the same mistakes over and over. We've got to get off the merry-go-round of "it's not my fault," and allow hardship to do its work to grow us up.

Running Low? Involve Jesus

Jesus went to a wedding with His disciples and His mom. This was at the very beginning of Jesus' ministry. Now, Jesus was just there as a guest, enjoying a wedding. In the course of the celebration, they ran out of wine. This was a big deal, so Jesus' mom went to Jesus and said, "They have no more wine," which was her way of telling Him she wanted Him to fix the problem. She knew He could do something about it. Jesus replied, "Dear woman, why do involve me?" (John 2:4). Now did His mom answer the question He asked? Nope, she looked at the wedding employees and said, "Do whatever he tells you" (John 2:5), which was her way of saying, "Hook it up, Jesus." It appears Jesus wasn't planning on getting involved until His mother she asked. In your life, you may run out of something like joy, health, or gas. Seriously, what do you run out of? Did you think to ask Jesus to help? Involve Jesus, and then when you do, remember to do whatever He says.

It's His Body

Ephesians 1:22-23 says, "God placed all things under his (Jesus') feet and appointed him to be head over everything for the church, which is his body." Jesus is in charge of the church, which is His body. Well, if the church is His body, it must be important to go to church. I mean, no matter how you might want to define church, we must recognize that this letter to the Ephesians was addressed to the church in Ephesus, which was a physical church where people worshipped God. Sometimes, Christians get in the habit of not going to church. Now, don't get mad at me for pointing this out, but church is important. In John 15, Christ repeatedly tells us to remain in Him, and we will produce fruit. He says apart from Him, we will produce nothing. As Christians, we want to produce fruit. To do that, we must come together with His body—the church—to worship and to hear the Word. It's a time of unification. Certainly we are all different and like different things, and so like siblings, we will argue a bit, but God is bringing us together toward Christ. This unification enhances our ability to grow. Now, I know all about the folks who say the church isn't relevant or is just full of hypocrites or whatever. Well, instead of bashing church, let's take some responsibility and get involved to help the church reach the world. Let's unite under our common faith in Jesus Christ. After all, it is His body.

To Tell the Truth

"Liar, liar pants on fire." I'm sure you've heard that before. Now, I have no idea why someone would think your pants would catch fire if you lie. I've never actually seen it happen: *Hey- what happened to your jeans? Well, I was telling my boss why I was late, and* boom, *my pants caught fire.* I actually just think it just rhymes; that's why they say it. But no one can deny, we are a society of truth stretching and exaggeration, or sometimes we lie by leaving things out of the story. Our little stretches and exaggerations mess with people's ability to trust us, especially those closest to you. For instance, when you tell your friends, "Oh, just tell Jimmy that I'm not feeling well," your friends tell Jimmy that, and then they think, "Hey, you're a liar." Then, when we are really telling the truth, we say, "No really, I promise, I swear," which is letting everyone know that normally you lie, but not this time. Now, I'm not trying to get down on you, but I do want you to hear this. Jesus said to not do all this promising stuff. He said in Matthew 5:37, "Simply let your 'Yes' be 'Yes,' and your 'No', 'No'." He's teaching us about truth. Let every word you speak be the truth as you know it, even if it means getting yourself in trouble. Then watch as you begin to grow.

Take Some Responsibility

On television the other day, I heard some people ask the question, "If there is a God, why is there world hunger?" I thought to myself, *Isn't it just like mankind to blame God for our problems?* The Israelites were led out of slavery into the desert and on the journey, they became angry. God had taken them out of slavery and was taking them to a good land, flowing with milk and honey. But their disobedience and unbelief made the journey to that land take longer than it should, so the people got all mad at Moses and God. Some things still haven't changed. Today in our world, there is all kinds of suffering and sometimes people get mad at God for what they are going through. But God is love. He sent His Son that we might have life and life more abundantly. It is the devil who comes to steal, kill and destroy, and often mankind helps him do his dirty work. Psalm 115:16 says "The highest heavens belong to the LORD, but the earth he has given to man." God has asked us to manage this planet, to steward over it, to rule over it. He asked us to take dominion and authority over it. So if there is world hunger, we better get to feeding the people. Don't forget, we are the hands and feet of Christ. When He wants to get something done, He needs man to obey. Let's be accountable for this world's troubles, and let's get to work on fixing them. Donate some money above your tithes to missions work in your church. Volunteer in your local community. Get involved. Get to work. Let's be faithful with this planet, it's our responsibility!!

Bad News

You hear it constantly: Gas prices are rising. This makes lots of other prices rise. The doom and gloom from the news media continues. Well, I've got no doom or gloom for you today. God's Word teaches us to focus on the good, not the bad. It says to speak good and to think positive and to expect the promises of God to be working in us and through us. God's Word shows me that it was during a great famine that Abraham, Isaac, and Joseph became wealthy. We are God's people. Don't let your thoughts or attitude be affected by the reports of famine in your land. The Bible says in Colossians 2:20, "Since you died with Christ to the basic principles of this world, why, as though you still belonged to it, do you submit to its rules?" As Christians, we are not subject to the circumstances, but we are rulers over circumstance. When a storm came up on Jesus, He didn't say, "Oh no, it's rain. I hope we're gonna make it." He took authority over the circumstance. He has given that same authority to us, but we set ourselves up to lose when we focus on the bad news. Don't let the sadness of the Wall Street Journal be in you. Instead, let the joy of the Lord be your strength. When you receive Christ, you enter the Kingdom of God. He has a different set of rules, and His streets are paved with gold. So you could just sell some pavement to buy some gas!

Real Food

At my daughter's birthday party, there must have been thirty people at my house. It takes a lot of food to feed all those people. The Bible tells us in John 6 that a huge crowd had gathered to see Jesus at dinner time. There were 5,000 men and then some women and children. Now, these people had apparently not planned ahead for dinner. There were no picnic baskets or sandwiches, so Jesus set out to feed them all. The only one who brought some food was a boy. Well, Jesus prayed over the five loaves of bread and two fish that the boy had with him, and the food went out and fed everyone and there was food left over. We should note that these were not starving refugees experiencing some sort of famine or a dire need to eat. They had just shown up without food. So why was it so important for Jesus to feed them? He fed them because He cared about them, but also, I think He was pleased at the real reason all these people had come out to see Him. They had come to hear Him teach. Jesus wishes to feed all of us, not barley and fish, but the Word of God. That is more important to our life and happiness than regular food, but are we eating? You've probably thought about what kind of food you'll eat today, but have you planned on eating some Word today? Grab yourself a Bible or a podcast and get some bread in you every day. The Word is what changes and grows us. The Bible has the wisdom you need for everything you will face.

Get the News Out

In Mark 16:15, Jesus said, "Go into all the world and preach the good news to all creation." What's the good news? The good news is that salvation is free to anyone who will accept Jesus Christ as the Son of God who died for all sin and make Him Lord and Savior of their life. Jesus told us to preach this good news to all creation. For some, that may mean traveling to Zimbabwe, but if everyone goes to Zimbabwe, then who is going to spread the good news in your neighborhood? I know a recent trend in society is to say that each person's faith is a private thing and so we shouldn't try to impose our faith on another. You know, let people believe what they want to believe. I want to caution you to be careful of this kind of thinking. Jesus instructed us to tell others about Him. Now, I'm not saying that we should all be at the street corner yelling at somebody driving by, saying he is destined to burn forever. What I'm saying is that people need to hear that God loves them and He sent His only Son to die for them. To many, God is this far away person who is randomly mean to the world. People need to hear that God is good and that He wants to be our Father, if we will receive Him. People need to hear about the difference Jesus has made in you. Ask God to give you an opportunity to share the good news. Give to others, love others, and soon doors will begin to open for you to share and be obedient to this command Jesus has given us.

Know Who You Are

Romans 8:16 says that the Spirit himself testifies with our spirit that we are God's children. Galatians 3:26 says, "You are all sons of God through faith in Christ Jesus." Think of what this means! Of all the people running the show on this planet, the kings, prime ministers, presidents or whatever, those world leaders cannot compare to the authority of God who is the Creator of all. And you, my friend, are a child of God! Now if you're the president's kid, you probably get some special privileges, right? You probably get free White House tours and Secret Service protection. If you're the son of a king or daughter of a king, that would make you a prince or a princess. Keep in mind, Jesus isn't just a king, He's the King of kings, according to Revelation chapter 19. Billy Graham was once asked if he gets nervous meeting with so many world leaders. His reply was, "I just remember that I am an ambassador for the greatest King of all, so there is no need to be nervous." Wherever you go, remember that you are royalty in the Kingdom of God and that you represent the Most High. God doesn't just call you royalty, He treats you like royalty. He is a great Father who gives the richest blessings to His children.

He Wants You

Do you ever look back at the things you've done wrong and think, *How can God use me, or why would He even want to?* Well, I want to encourage you today. In Matthew 1, the lineage of Jesus Christ is listed from Abraham to Joseph. In that lineage are plenty of people who made huge mistakes. David, the man after God's own heart, stole another man's wife and then had the man bumped off. But God used and blessed David. One of the women mentioned in the lineage of Jesus was involved in prostitution, but she was used mightily by God. Now this doesn't mean we should go on sinning. Sin has consequences in this world. But God used these people and many more who made mistakes. So what have you done? Religion might tell you that God can only use that church dude who is squeaky clean, but believe me, God has used and continues to use anyone who will just say, "OK!" Proverbs 2:8 says, "He (God) guards the course of the just." No one is just on his own, but by faith in Jesus Christ, you have been justified, which makes you just. God is now guarding your course, so get on your course and run because God has confidence in you. He's not looking for squeaky clean, He's looking for someone to say, "OK!" Is that you?

Passion Isn't Enough

Proverbs 19:2 says, "It is not good to have zeal without knowledge." "Zeal" simply means to be really excited about something to the point that you are driven to act on it. Here, God is saying that before you start acting on all that zeal, you need to learn everything you can about what you're so excited about. If you're playing basketball with tons of passion and heart but you don't know the rules, then you could cause your team to lose. God wants you to be zealous about the Lord, but He is also asking you to learn His ways so that you can share about Him with excellence. When people are seeking God, they often do so by asking questions. You need to know the answers! Now if I wanted to learn about basketball, I would read books and attend basketball camps. If I were serious about it, I would join a team. To learn God's ways, we must read His Word, join a church where we can grow in the Lord, and allow the Holy Spirit within us to lead us into the truth. So get studied up! The test is coming and to win, you are going to need passion, knowledge and God's wisdom.

We Are Family

Do you like everyone in your family all the time? Do you ever fight within your family? Have you ever been to a family reunion and met people you didn't know you were related to? Sometimes we meet relatives and we are surprised we're related. God defines His people as a family. In Ephesians 2:19, it says that we are all members of God's household. That's right, we're family. So when you go to church, there will probably be people you don't always get along with. You may clash. Ladies, someone is bound to say, "Wow, you look tired" or some other hurtful thing. But we are family and what is awesome about family is that deep down inside, we are united. Don't let division come in to your family, but embrace that unity God is calling us to. My brother and I were fighting once and my friend started in on my brother. What did I do? I was like, "Excuse me, that's *my* brother. Don't talk to *my* brother like that." Don't leave your church because your feelings get hurt, but instead be reconciled to your brothers and sisters. Be united and love like the family we are.

Stand Out from the Crowd

In grade school, I was the short kid, which means I got teased. I didn't like standing out because I was "vertically challenged." From our childhood, most of us are trained to blend with the crowd. Less than two months after the Israelites left Egypt, Moses came down from Mount Sinai with a whole slew of rules for the Israelites. Don't do this; stop doing that. You see the Israelites had been living in Egypt for 430 years, so they had Egyptian habits and Egyptian ways of thinking. They looked, acted, and smelled like Egypt. God wanted to distinguish the Israelites from the world. He wanted them to be different. Christians are to be different from the world. Before we met Christ, we did as the world did, but now as a Christian, we are supposed to stand out. We should live differently, give differently, love differently, act differently and our life should smell differently. While the world may hate, we forgive. While they hate their enemies, we pray for ours. This is a different way of thinking. The world may see us as crazy, but we're just different. We stand out, just like our Father wants us to.

Knowing God

How can we know God and be saved? Where will we spend eternity? You were made by God to be His, but you can choose to reject God. We reject Him by not seeking Him. How do we seek and find God? Jesus explained to His followers that no one can come to the Father except through Him. Many people think believing in God is enough, but even Satan believes in God. Others think we can be good enough on our own, but then how good is good enough and who can live perfectly anyway? Jesus sacrificed His life so that by believing in Him, you can be made perfect and you can know God. So is today your day? You can know God today and be saved. Romans 10:9 says, "That if you confess with your mouth, 'Jesus is Lord,' and believe in your heart that God raised him from the dead, you will be saved." Ask God to forgive you of your sins and ask Jesus to be Lord of your life. Say it out loud. Now, go find a good church. There is much to learn and we need you on the team!

Potential

In science class, you learned potential energy is how much energy is stored. You and I have potential in us. If I asked you what your potential is, I would get many different answers. A great way to determine what you really think of your potential would be to measure the size of your dreams. How big can you see? When Abraham was believing God for just one son, God took him outside and showed him the vastness of the night sky. He told him that his offspring would be as numerous as the stars. He was saying to Abraham, "Dream bigger, don't just believe Me for one son. Let's expand your horizons." Sometimes we lower our sights so that we aren't let down. And people aren't always helpful in encouraging our dreams. The world's message is that you can't, that you aren't smart enough or that God isn't interested in blessing you. But God's message is that He has blessed you, that the same Spirit that raised Christ from the dead dwells in you, and you can do all things through Christ who strengthens you. Stop believing what the world says about you and believe what God says. After all, He created you so He would know best!

Building the Inside

I think my favorite part of going to the beach is building sand castles with my kids. We may take it a bit too seriously, but with our shovels and pails we take hours building the castle, the walls, the living quarters and moat. It's a whole kingdom. In Luke 17:20-21, Jesus explains, "The kingdom of God does not come with your careful observation, nor will people say, 'Here it is' or 'There it is,' because the kingdom of God is within you." Many of us spend a great deal of time trying to build a life around us. But the real building that needs to take place is within us. God wants to build His kingdom within you where the cornerstone is Jesus Christ. His Word is the blueprint. This is going to strengthen what is on the inside of you so when the waves on the outside crash against you, all the troubles that this world and the thief bring, you will remain strong and unshakeable. Don't worry so much about the outside, focus on what's being built inside you. Study the Word, get connected to the church, and let the strength God gives you from within bring you victory.

Having Jesus in the Boat

In Mark 6:45, we see that Jesus was ashore while the disciples were rowing a boat across the lake to Bethsaida. They started rowing just after dinnertime and they were still rowing at the fourth watch of the night. The Word of God says that they were straining at the oars because the wind was against them. They rowed and rowed nearly all night, probably 10 hours, while getting nowhere. Have you ever felt like this in life? Like you were trying and trying, but going nowhere? You were tired and up in the all-night of your life, straining at the oars with the wind against you. Quitting is not the answer, but there is an answer. Jesus came walking out on the water past the disciples. They cried out to Him and He got in the boat. Now watch this: It says in verse 51, "Then He climbed into the boat with them, and the wind died down." Jesus is the Prince of Peace and when He got in the boat, peace came. This didn't mean they didn't have to row anymore, but suddenly the rowing got a whole lot easier. If you are rowing and tired, it may be that you have forgotten to have Jesus in your boat. Let Him bring you peace today. May the Lord of Peace give you peace.

He Sympathizes with Our Weaknesses

Have you ever been tempted to do something you know you shouldn't? Well, did you do it? You lied, didn't you? Stole? Cheated? Coveted? Envied? Judged? Hebrews 4:15 says, "For we do not have a high priest who is unable to sympathize with our weaknesses." God made you. God knows you better than anyone. He knows that like Adam, when we mess up, we hide from Him. Hey, guess what? Your weaknesses are not a surprise to Him. Jesus walked this earth so He understands temptation. In fact, it says here He sympathizes with our weaknesses. Sympathy is not judgment, and it is not anger. When we offer someone sympathy, we are offering them support and telling them that everything is going to be okay. Jesus is sympathizing with our weaknesses. This doesn't mean you can have a sinfest; instead, allow Christ's forgiveness to wash over you, and let His grace teach you to be godly. Don't let your shame separate you from God. Say, "Hey Jesus, I messed up, please forgive me." Now ask God to give you strength to overcome, quit trying to do it on your own! God can help—He wants to help.

Juice

Have you heard the latest juice yet? Juice is when we talk bad about others, revel in their failures, or share what someone else said, but only when they are not around. The stories get bigger because, you know, we have to make it interesting, so we may add little bits in here and there. Proverbs 16:28 says, "A perverse man stirs up dissension, and a gossip separates close friends." Well, I don't want to be perverse. But, sometimes I do it. I get out my spoon and stir up a big pot of dissension. All of this creates drama in our lives, which will eventually come back to us. What you are sowing, you get to reap—like hurt friends and broken relationships. The best prescription to cure dissension is love. Love doesn't advertise sin. The Word of God teaches that love covers over a multitude of sins. When you choose to love, you walk away from these conversations. When someone digs for juice, you speak kindly of others with understanding. You strive to see the best in others. That's going to bring a harvest you'll be glad to reap.

Super Power

If I were going to be a superhero, I think I would be the Incredible Hulk. I'm little and white, so I think it would be neat to be big and green for a few minutes every now and then. I don't want the angry part though, but I do like the power. The Hulk is powerful. But, what does he need all that power for? I mean, what is the purpose of being powerful? Colossians 1:11 says that you are "being strengthened with all power according to his glorious might." So God gives you power, which gives you strength. Now why would God give you power and strength? God wants His children to have victory, so He gives you power because He knows there will be some fighting to do. Sometimes you might get beat up a little, but with God's power, you get back up. When you get tired in the fight, you need to draw upon God's power. That power will give you strength and then you will be like the Hulk, except you won't be all green or angry. Instead you will be happy and you will have great endurance, patience, and victory.

What Do You Do with Your Time?

Time is valuable. Ephesians 5:16 speaks of "redeeming the time, because the days are evil" (NKJV). Well, I'll agree. The days do seem a bit evil. I mean, I think we can agree that this world needs some help. But what does it mean to redeem time? Well, *redeem* refers to an exchange for something of value. Jesus redeemed us, which shows how much He values us. So redeeming time means God wants us to take every moment we have and make it valuable. The last moment that just passed, was it productive? God is asking us to use our time to make the days less evil. That would mean spending time investing in your future, your children, or expanding God's kingdom. What kinds of things do we do that are a waste of time? I think sometimes we Christians are sitting when there is a race to be run! There is a lot to be done here on this planet. It's important that we find a way to stay productive for God's kingdom.

Laughing for Success

Have you ever laughed so hard that your stomach hurt or tears came out of your eyes? When you were done, was your face tired from smiling? God gave us laughter. It is a gift for expressing how we feel. We were made in God's likeness, which means God laughs too. Proverbs 31:25 is describing a successful woman, and it says "She can laugh at the days to come." Now I don't know what is going to happen tomorrow. It could be great or it could be terrible. But worrying about it won't help. My outlook on tomorrow affects how I feel today. Instead of being happy today, I could be down worrying what tomorrow holds. God is saying when we think about tomorrow, we should chuckle. Maybe we should even be thinking, *Yeah, tomorrow is going to be a great day! I'm not worried or afraid of tomorrow, I'm excited about it. It will be an even better day than today.* The Bible describes a woman who is so excited about the future, it makes her laugh. We get the idea that even if she had something big coming up, she was expecting to have victory in whatever battle was approaching. Let's follow her lead and approach tomorrow with laughter.

The Right Decision, Every Time

What if every decision you made starting right now was the right decision? It would be like taking a test in school and you answer every question perfectly. In life, sometimes I don't come to a fork in the road. I come to an intersection with 50 different directions I can go. So which direction is the right one? What if in every situation, you made the right decision? One key to success is the ability to make good decisions, and the key to making right decisions is having the right information. In I Samuel 30, David was in a tough situation. His family and the families of his army had been kidnapped, his stuff had been stolen, and his camp burned. What was David to do? Well, David inquired of the Lord and got his answer. As a result, everyone and everything was restored to him and his army. God has the right kind of information and He has stored it all up for you in one book. It's the most printed book in all of history. This book has God's kind of information. Do you need direction or wisdom? Read the greatest book of wisdom ever. Inquire of the Lord today. He knows exactly what to do.

Reading God's Diary

Digging through some old boxes the other day, I came across my wife's old diary. She gave me the green light to read through it, and it was such an eye opener. As well as I know my wife after years of marriage, it was still so insightful to read her innermost thoughts and feelings. Sometimes I'd get to a page and I wouldn't quite understand what she was saying, but she sat right there with me as I read so I could ask her, "Hey, what were you saying right here?" I really learned a lot that day about her. It brought me a great deal of understanding. I really saw how much she loves me. I thought about how the Bible is just like that. It is God's diary—His love story with us. The next time I was reading my Bible, I thought about that. I was reading God's personal and intimate love letter to us. And every time I read, He is right there with me. I can ask Him, "Hey, what did You mean right here?" as I point to a scripture. God may answer through my life experience or I might remember another scripture like it that clears up my questions. Or, I may hear a gentle voice inside of me giving me wisdom. God wants you to know Him, so read His diary, and then ask Him to make His heart known to you.

Healing Touch

In Acts 28:8, Paul was staying with a local official whose father was sick in bed suffering from fever and dysentery. Paul went in to see him and, after prayer, he placed his hands on him and healed him. Healing was a recurring theme in Jesus' earthly ministry. He would often pray for others who were sick and would place His hands on them to heal them. Once, a woman in a crowd simply touched the clothing of Jesus and was healed. Now I don't understand exactly how my computer works, but I do know that I have to turn it on to make it work. In prayer, the laying on of hands works. Something happens in our prayer when we join together. We are physical creatures, and that touch with prayer means something. In our society, that touch may seem weird, some might even tease about it because it seems strange. Still, when I pray for someone, I will follow this pattern that Jesus laid out for us since I know that it works. You have the Spirit of the Lord in you so the next time you're praying for someone, grab a hand, touch the hem of a garment or a shoulder or forehead and believe God is greater, then see the salvation of your God.

Help in Deep Water

Have you ever been in the deep waters of life where it can be dark and cold? Ever had a rough day, rough week, rough month? I have, too. Someone will ask, "So, how are you?" and you don't know what else to say so you respond, "Umm, okay I guess." David, before he became king, was hunted by King Saul. That had to be rough. In 2 Samuel 22:17, David was singing a song about that time in his life. He speaks of God saying, "He reached down from on high and took hold of me; he drew me out of deep waters." Yeah, maybe the water is deep, but it is never too deep for God. Besides, without a little deep water how would we ever learn to swim? David goes on singing, "You give me your shield of victory; you stoop down to make me great" (v. 36). While you're keeping your head above water, do you know what God is doing? He is getting you out! What a great truth! God wants you to be great. He has even given you His shield of victory, so when God wins, you win. So keep swimming and get ready to be great!

Through the Fire

In Isaiah 43:2, God says, "When you pass through the waters, I will be with you; and when you pass through the rivers, they will not sweep over you. When you walk through the fire, you will not be burned." Wow, you are protected, aren't you? God is with you. Sometimes people get the idea that God is far away, but He isn't. He's right here with you. When you travel through the drive-thru, He is there. He is there when you are making dinner or going to work. He is with you. He said that when you go through the fire, you won't get burned. In Daniel 3, Shadrach Meshach and Abednego were thrown into the fire for doing the right thing. Sometimes making good decisions and standing for what is right land us in the fiery furnace. God didn't say there wouldn't be any fire. He said you wouldn't get burned. After Shadrach, Meshach and Abednego were thrown in, the king looked into the fiery furnace and saw four people there instead of three. Yeah, even in the fire, He is with you. Because of this truth, maybe being in the fire isn't all that bad because you're with God. Since you know He is right there, you might as well talk to Him. Besides, He knows just what to do.

Hope

Jesus came to preach good news. You know what good news does? It gives us hope. I like hope. Hope feels good. I think everyone likes hope, but not everyone hopes. Sometimes we even talk about the worst-case scenario so that we don't get hopeful. After all, we don't want to be let down. Listen to what God says in Romans 5:5, "And hope does not disappoint us, because God has poured out his love into our hearts by the Holy Spirit." The message of Christ—the good news—is hopeful. It says you are a child of God and a joint heir with Christ. It says no weapon formed against you can win and that God desires to bless you, to bring you peace, to heal anything in your life that needs healing. These are hopeful statements. Does God desire to bring you hope? Yes, and you don't have to be worried about being disappointed when it comes to God's hope. God's kind of hope does not disappoint. This world will disappoint you, but God will not. His promises are always true.

What Would You Do?

Have you heard the advertising catch phrase, "What would you do for a Klondyke bar?" It's asking what you would be willing to do for the pleasure of eating that chocolaty, ice cream goodness. This is an age-old question. It reminds me of when my brother would say, "Hey, I'll give you $1 to drink Tabasco sauce." (Which, by the way, he still owes me that dollar!) Drinking Tabasco and working for a Klondyke bar are innocent enough activities. However, Satan and the world will offer you all sorts of pleasure in return for things that you know are wrong. At what point do we decide to do what is right, no matter what the exchange or how good that Klondyke bar looks? In Matthew 16:26, Jesus said it this way, "What good will it be for a man if he gains the whole world, yet forfeits his soul?" It's not that God wants us to live life without pleasures. He promised His children a land flowing with milk and honey. But we must determine in our hearts to not fall for the enemy's shortcuts to pleasure along the journey to God's promise. We must be willing to hold out for the good things of God and believe that He who has promised is faithful!

Channel Surfing

People lose interest in a TV show and turn the channel. Who cares? It's just a sitcom. But life is not a sitcom, yet our society is training us to change channels on anything in life that is getting boring. God has designed specific things in our lives to last, like our marriage. He describes marriage as a covenant. When a couple first gets married, everything is so perfect. On the wedding day, if you ask each person "Is this the perfect person for you," each would say yes. But speaking from my own experience, after I got married, my wife suddenly found out that I'm not perfect. I know, hard to believe. So should she just change the channel? *No*, because marriage is a covenant. Marriage brings with it extremely amazing and happy times. You have an intimate friend who shares everything with you. But what about the low times? Is this when we throw in the towel? *No*, the low times are when we dig in our roots, get them down deep, and we grow. So put down your remote and get committed to making it work. Then watch the joy of the Lord fill you with strength!

What to Do

Have you ever heard about someone else's sin? What do we do with that information? Well, we could tell our friends, but then, that doesn't seem right. Or we could hold the information in our heart and say, "Well, that wasn't godly." I know—we could send out a well-worded tweet on the Internet. But let me ask you, have you ever done something that you wouldn't want announced from the rooftops? First John 1:8 says, "If we claim to be without sin, we deceive ourselves and the truth is not in us." Sometimes when we see someone else's mess, it makes us feel better about our own. We think, *I'd never do that.* But this scripture is a reminder that we all mess up so when another Christian stumbles, we need to remember our humanity. Now, I'm not saying that sin does not need to be addressed, but consider how it needs to be addressed. Jesus redeemed us from sin with His blood. First John 1:9 says, "If we confess our sins, He is faithful and just and will forgive us our sins and purify us from all unrighteousness." When we judge others who sin, the irony is that we have reacted in a sinful way. It is better for us to say, "Well I haven't got it all together either, but praise God for the blood of the Lamb." Hallelujah, Amen.

Our Helper

In John 14, Jesus was explaining to the disciples that He would be leaving soon, and they were a little freaked out. Jesus said in verse 16, "And I will pray the Father, and He will give you another Helper, that He may abide with you forever" (NKJV). Later, He explained that this Helper is the Holy Spirit. After Jesus died and was resurrected, before He returned to heaven, He instructed the disciples, "Do not leave Jerusalem, but wait for the gift my Father promised, which you have heard me speak about. For John baptized with water, but in a few days you will be baptized with the Holy Spirit" (Acts 1:4-5). In Acts 2, we see this happen. They were all baptized in the Holy Spirit. Well, 2000 years later, this promise is still for us, since Jesus said the Helper would be with us forever. Now I don't know about you, but I sometimes need a little help. Things come up that I cannot deal with in my own strength. When you need help, ask God for the Holy Spirit, and the Spirit will bring help. The Holy Spirit is available to anyone who has received Christ. Study in the Word about the Holy Spirit, and watch the God of our salvation transform your life.

Blessed

"Sticks and stones will break my bones but words will never hurt me." You may think that's in the Bible, but it's not. But here is something that is. In Luke 6:22, it says, "Blessed are you when men hate you, when they exclude you and insult you, and reject your name as evil, because of the Son of Man." Have you ever been hated? Rejected? Had someone call you names? Trust me when I say Jesus knows how you feel. Back in Jesus' day, there was a lot of division between those who followed Christ and those who did not. In those times, if a Jew chose to believe in Jesus, he faced rejection from family and friends. There were even people, like Saul, who went around killing Christians. Two thousand years later, it seems that there are still many out there throwing verbal stones against faith in Christ by making fun of Christians. No one likes to be hated. For this reason, Jesus encourages us. It's encouraging to know that Jesus knew this would happen, and even more encouraging to know that when it happens, Jesus says we are blessed. That's why we can walk in forgiveness. Praise God, who turns all things around for the good of those who serve Him.

Being Used

In Mark 14, there is a famous story of the girl who poured perfume on Jesus. In this story, the girl was criticized because the perfume she poured out could have been sold and the money given to the poor. The perfume she used was a lot more expensive than the Old Spice I use. It was worth a year's wages. In today's economy, we would say the perfume cost about 30,000 bucks. That's some crazy good smelling stuff, you know. While others were criticizing the girl, Jesus said that she had poured perfume on His body to prepare for His burial. I'm just guessing, but I don't think she knew it wouldn't be long before He was crucified. Here is a woman who felt compelled to do this good act and was used by God in this mighty way, probably without understanding the special way God was using her. She is still remembered today for doing this great thing. Isn't it awesome to know that as you go through life, if you will make yourself available to the Lord, He may be using you in enormously mighty ways? He is acting out His most perfect plan all while you are unaware, simply following a compulsion to act out in love. So when man criticizes you, God is proud of you, saying, "Well done My good and faithful servant."

First

Don't we always believe that first is best? God is first and He is best. God gave His very best, His one and only Son for us. He is the biggest, strongest, fastest, and smartest. He is God. God thinks highly of firsts. He has asked us to give to Him our first fruits, which means, our very best. A farmer's first fruits are the strongest of the crop that is harvested that season. God wants to have first place in your heart so that He can carry out His first and best plan for your life. He has mapped out a race for you and wants you to win first place. In all of this, sometimes we still walk this earth feeling inadequate, weak, and defeated. There are those of us who feel ugly, or slow, or like me, just a bit on the short side. But God does not do things in a second-place manner. He doesn't cut corners or settle for mediocre. When He made you, He took His time and He shaped you with His own hands. You are important to Him and He absolutely and completely designed you as the best. He has placed His strength within you and given you the mind of Christ. You are beautiful. Be encouraged today to know that God has created you, and He makes good stuff!

Treasures

I have a closet full of stuff, half of which I never wear. I have a garage full of totes, some of which I have no idea what is inside. As each year goes by, these things get dustier and degrade. Jesus said, "Do not store up for yourselves treasures on earth, where moth and rust destroy, and where thieves break in and steal. But store up for yourselves treasures in heaven" (Matthew 6:19-20). Well, my "treasures" in my garage aren't really treasures at all and they need to be cleaned out and given away. But it is interesting to hear about heavenly treasure. According to Christ, there is treasure. We work all day for a paycheck, but how much of it lasts? I'll bet if we could see what our obedience to God, our love for and kind words to others, and our gifts to the Lord were adding to our storage space in heaven, we would take our Christian game up a level. "Hey, I forgave someone and scored a gold mailbox!" Now, I am just having fun with this, but we should be aware that God will reward you, not man, and that His reward is way cooler and will last forever. Now get out there and get some treasure in heaven!

Share Your Boat, Put Out Your Nets

In Luke 5, Jesus was teaching by a lake and the crowd was pressing in on Him a bit, so He sat down in a man's boat and asked the man to put out to sea just a little. From there, Jesus kept teaching. When He had finished teaching, He asked the man to put out into deep water and let down the nets for a catch. Now, it was Simon who owned the boat. Simon explained that he and his partners had been fishing all night and there were no fish. But then he said that since Jesus had asked, he would obey. Well, they brought in a huge catch; more than the nets could hold. You see, when you give to Jesus, you should get ready to be blessed. Even when everything you have been trying has not been working, when you obey God, the blessings will come. God wants to give to you, like He did Simon, more than your nets can hold. What was the key to Simon's blessing? He was ready to give, and ready to obey. Now get out your nets and hold on!

What Does Your Face Say?

The other day, I was with my friend who said, "Hey, is everything okay?" I said, "Yeah, it's great." Then he said, "Oh, you just seem a bit down." Well I wasn't down, but the fact that my friend thought I was got me to thinking. Isaiah 61:9 says, "All who see them will acknowledge that they are a people the LORD has blessed." That "they" means us. This verse says that everyone who sees us will acknowledge that God is blessing us. How will they know God is blessing us just by seeing us? Well, if we walk around looking down and out, then no one is going to think we're blessed. We are redeemed, but we have to let our smiles say so. I also thought about how Jesus said that we are the light of the world, and that a light is not to be hidden (Matthew 5:14-16). As people see us walking around looking down and discouraged, we're saying that we're not happy and not blessed. That's not what we want to say. We want the whole world to know by our faces that God is blessing us. So when someone asks, "Why are you smiling," you can say, "Because God has so blessed me."

What's in Your Heart?

What is in your heart? Memories are in your heart. People you love and things you think or believe are also in your heart. In Luke 6, Jesus teaches that our heart can contain good stuff and sometimes it contains bad stuff. Verse 45 says, "The good man brings good things out of the good stored up in his heart, and the evil man brings evil things out of the evil stored up in his heart." So it's clear that if we want good stuff coming out, we've got to get some good stuff inside. Now, television isn't always loading up your heart with good, and sometimes you may find yourself feeling all out of love, with no joy left to give. You need a "good stuff in your heart" recharge. The best tool for getting good in your heart (and the bad stuff out) is described in Hebrews 4:12. It says, "For the word of God is living and active. Sharper than any double-edged sword, it penetrates even to dividing soul and spirit, joints and marrow; it judges the thoughts and attitudes of the heart." That's right. Studying God's Word rewrites the stories in your heart and it begins to change how you think and also changes your attitude, which is another term for how you feel. So grab some Word of God today and allow it to shape what's stored in that heart of yours.

What You Were Doesn't Matter

What did you do yesterday? Was it good? Bad? Do anything you regret? Second Timothy 1:9 tells us that God has "called us to a holy life—not because of anything we have done but because of his own purpose and grace." First, notice that God has called you; that is exciting. You might be thinking, *Me?* Yea, He has called you. Next, notice that He has called you to a holy life. "Holy" means to be set apart for God's purposes. God chose you for His purposes. You might ask, "Why would He choose me? I mess up, I have some skeletons in my closet, and years ago I did this or that." Well, the verse says that He did not call you because of anything you have done, but instead because of His own purpose and grace. God's grace is served up to you to remove all your mess-ups. Jesus' blood provides this. God calls you exactly as you are. The sometimes-not-so-perfect you is perfected for God's plans. So whatever is in your past, give it to God, let it go, forget about it. Today is a brand new day. Don't let who you used to be stop you from becoming who God says that you can be.

Who Is God?

In Hosea 12:9, God says, "I am the LORD your God, who brought you out of Egypt." In the days of Hosea, people believed in lots of different gods, so God made sure to identify Himself by first saying "I am the Lord" (you know, in charge, the real deal). Next, He identifies Himself as, "Your God." Here, He's saying that He is OURS, which would in turn mean that we are His. Then He further clarifies who He is by reminding the people of something amazing He did—"who brought you out of Egypt." God wants to remind you today that He has done huge things in your life. He even brought you out of your Egypt. Remember, we were all slaves to our flesh and sin before we received Christ. He wants you to remember, however, that not only is He the source of your past miracle, but He also has some great things in store for your future. He is your God—*yours*—which means He is the source of your strength and the answer to the impossible problems in your life. Remember today who God is, that He is yours, remember something He's done, and now praise Him for what He is about to do.

Energized!

Doing the right thing doesn't always seem all that fun—things like praying for enemies, forgiving, and turning the other cheek. God never promised that doing the right thing would be easy or fun. If it were, then everyone would do it. But doing the right thing always leads to life. Sometimes, people get tired of doing right. Isaiah 40:29 says, "He gives strength to the weary, and increases the power of the weak." God knows you, and He knows that sometimes you might get tired of pushing on, believing for the miracle, standing on the Word, and praying and asking for help. But what other options are there? Either you quit trying or you try harder. God promises that when you hit some discouragement, He will give you strength and increase your power. Now, why would He do that? Does He give you strength and power so that you can give up? So that you can be defeated? Nope. He's giving you just what you need to win, because on the other side of this weariness is a win. God is spurring you onward with persever-ance and strength. You thought a cup of coffee was a jolt of energy? Ask God to come through and energize you in every way.

How to Defeat Temptation

In Matthew 4, we read that Jesus had been in the wilderness for 40 days when Satan came along to tempt Him. That's just what Satan likes to do. He likes to tempt. Four thousand years after tempting Adam and Eve with the fruit, he was up to his same old tricks. Do you know why Satan likes to tempt? I do. It's because it works. It gets us off track and distracted from our race. And the reason temptation works is because sin is a great shortcut to fun. But the devil's kind of fun makes a mess of things and leaves us derailed in life. God invented happiness, but to find God's kind of happiness, we cannot give in to Satan's shortcuts. Did you notice what Jesus did when He was tempted? Every time the devil tempted him, Jesus answered with what God had to say about the situation. He quoted the Word of God. Jesus had His defenses up and strong. He had the sword of the spirit, which is the Word of God. When He had had all He was going to take from Satan, Jesus said, "Away from Me, Satan." Then, the devil left Him. Jesus has given you authority over Satan in His name. James 4:7 says, "Resist the devil, and he will flee from you." So today, say to Satan, "Oh no, I'm not falling for that again. Take a hike in Jesus' name."

The Sound of Music

Music is powerful. It has the ability to make us feel something, whether happy or sad or even energized for a work out. Songs make us remember things, take us new places in our minds, and get us dreaming. They make our feet tap or our hands want to clap. Now, God invented music and thousands of years before there was radio (or an iPod), there were the psalms. In Psalm 95:1, David sings, "Come, let us sing for joy to the LORD." I notice that in the psalms, no matter how David was feeling, whether he was up or down, winning or losing, David found a way to sing to God. Why is that? Well, a song can help you remember that God is your strength and it gets God involved in what you are doing. It can change how you feel. It can even get you ready to win. If you need a bit of joy, then sing for it. Sing with others, like at church. A bunch of people all singing to the Lord may be just the change you need this week.

Check the Fruit

Quickly, take an inventory of your friends. Jesus said in Matthew 7:17 that a good tree produces good fruit, and a bad tree produces bad fruit. He says you'll recognize a tree by its fruit. The "trees" here are people. Now don't judge your friends, but look at the fruit their lives produce. Jesus was teaching us in this passage that not everyone is doing the right thing. Of course, you already know that. But are your friends doing the right things? Do your friends pull you up, or drag you down? Are they calling you to do the right thing, work harder, and grow, or are they trying to get you to party, be lazy, and lose? You want to surround yourself with people who will spur you on. I can hear the arguments already: "Yeah but didn't Jesus hang out with the sinner?" He would minister to everyone, yes, but He hung out with His disciples. Likewise, it is important that we love everyone, as Jesus did, but be careful who you allow to influence your life. Not everyone is going to be a good influence for you. Pray and ask God that He might help you find good influences. Check the fruit. Look for good fruit to lead you to a great friend.

How's Your Foundation?

You've heard the children's song that encourages you to build your house on the rock so it will stand. Well, that song comes from Luke 6:47-49, where Jesus was describing two kinds of people. One person hears what God is asking him to do and then does it. He is building a house on the rock. The other fellow, well, he knows the right thing to do, but he does something else. Let's take for example tithing. Yeah, maybe God is asking him to tithe, but forget it. Or what about living with his girlfriend? He knows it's wrong, but it "feels so right." This man is building a life on the sand. Now both houses are going to be hit by a storm. That is normal and expected. Following Christ doesn't mean there won't be any more storms, it just means you'll see different results. The house built on the rock is fine after the storm. The house on the sand, well, it's not good. Everything that has been built suddenly falls apart in the storm. Obedience to God's Word is the key to whether your house will stand or fall. So whatever you have been doing in your life until now, choose to obey God right now. Get back on track and build your house on the rock.

God Bless You

In Genesis, we see a story that illustrates just how valuable it is to be blessed by God. It started on a day when Jacob, Isaac's younger son, was cooking some stew and Esau, Isaac's older son, came in from the field super hungry. Esau said, "Quick, let me have some of that red stew. I'm starving." Well, Jacob said, "I'll trade you some stew for your birthright." Now, this was a big deal, as Esau was basically giving up his inheritance. Esau said, "What good is the birthright to me if I starve to death?" Esau was not actually about to starve to death, yet he was willing to trade his inheritance for a moment of pleasure, letting his body tell him what to do. Esau didn't take the blessing seriously. Jacob, on the other hand, went through a lot to get the blessing in place of his older brother. Jacob saw the blessing as something worth fighting for. You and I make decisions every day, and so I ask, are we sometimes trading in God's best for us for a moment of pleasure? For something our body wants? Are we living our lives like Jacob, who valued the inheritance, or are we living like Esau, who traded it all in for stew?

What's Your Response?

Someday, someone is going to really tick you off. Now, I don't think it is because people are trying to be mean. I think it's because people are, well, people. We don't always act as we should, do we? From time to time, your brother may say something mean or your sister may get into your stuff. Mom and Dad may be in one of their moods, or your friends may turn their backs on you, or someone you don't even know may cut you off. A co-worker may throw you under the bus, or your spouse may chuck a pan at you. How are we going to be able to keep a good attitude through the day if everyone is making us mad? Proverbs 19:11 tells us that, "A man's wisdom gives him patience; it is to his glory to overlook an offense." Overlooking an offense means not getting all ticked off, but loving everyone around you regardless of what is going on. This kind of patience comes from wisdom, and it will be to your glory. So in the end, the biggest winner is the person who is smart enough to not get so worked up all the time, but who instead loves others, showing patience with everyone.

Faithful

In order to be great at something, you must first be faithful. Proverbs 28:20 says that a faithful man will be richly blessed. Proverbs 3:3 tells us to bind faithfulness and love around our necks and write them on the tablets of our hearts. So what does it mean to be faithful? Sometimes we can best understand a term by understanding its opposite. The opposite of faithful is faithless. To be faithless is to have no faith. Therefore, to be faithful is to be full of faith. This means being full of believing in God and what He has said. When right and wrong are in front of me, I should fully believe God and what He says about the situation. When fear tries to grip me and get me to quit, I should fully trust that God is my fortress and I can continue on in the race because I have remained full of faith. Likewise, when people wonder if you are scared or confused, you can confidently say, "No. I have bound faithfulness around my neck and I'm good to go."

Positivity

David, a man after God's own heart, was an optimist. An optimist is not an eye doctor, but a positive thinker. If you don't believe me, check out the psalms that he wrote. They reflect his thoughts, which were most often uplifting, joyful, and full of praise. Now sometimes David would start a song all down and feeling depressed, but in the end he would always be back up, happy, and feeling victorious. This is an example for us all. We need to stay positive and encouraged. When you are getting down, let your thoughts of God bring you back up. See the good in things, situations, and others. Whatever thoughts you focus on will stir emotions that go with those thoughts, and some nasty thinking can send you spiraling into despair. Instead, focus on what's good about today. Is the sun shining? Well if it is, then great. If it's cloudy, thank God for the shade. David learned to praise God, not just when things were great, but also when things were bad. You can't control everything, but you can control your thoughts and take them captive. You can keep your attitude good, lined up with God's Word, then you'll have a much better chance of enjoying your day, your family, your friends, and your life.

Aim High

Ever shoot a basketball? Ever miss the shot? Well, of course you have! Even the best basketball players in the world miss about half their shots. Were you aiming to miss? Of course not! You aim to make the shot. In 2 Corinthians 13:11, Paul says "aim for perfection." Well, perfection is a pretty lofty goal. Paul is saying to aim high. In our humanity, perfection is quite impossible. Paul wants us to aim for something that seems impossible. Often, life beats us up and we find ourselves aiming for just enough. Are we aiming for average? Are we shooting for mediocre? I think sometimes we aim low because we don't like to fail, but God is telling us to aim for the impossible, the improbable, the unseeable, the bull's-eye. He wants you to set your aim so high that everyone, including you, thinks that the only way you could possibly hit the mark is with the help of God. Aim for perfection, because with God all things are possible. Forget about your humanity and your tendencies to fall or fail, and remember that God is God and you are His child. Now dig deep and aim for the top!

Never Fail

I failed my first art class in college. It's true. I loved art too, so it was weird. In the grand scheme of my life, that failure hasn't really impacted me, except I have to occasionally own up to failing an art class. There, I said it. Walt Disney failed in his first media job because they said he wasn't creative enough. Paul admitted to his imperfections and failures. You have failed from time to time. Some failures don't really matter, but other failures in life can be devastating. In I Corinthians 13:8, God teaches us that "love never fails." What is it that empowered Jesus Christ to overcome all to defeat death and sin? It was love. Although my art class wasn't super important, there are things in my life that are important. If I want to be sure to win at those things, I must learn and grow in the one area that never fails—love. Specifically, God's kind of love. God's love gives. God's kind of love is always compelling you to an action, a sacrifice, a gift, a service to others. If you need a little victory in your life, try upping the love.

Things that Go Bump in the Night

Have you ever been trying to sleep when you hear some noise and your heart starts beating faster.... What was that? It's like your imagination takes over and you can almost picture someone creeping around outside. God said to the Israelites in Leviticus 26:6, "'I will grant peace in the land, and you will lie down and no one will make you afraid. I will remove savage beasts from the land, and the sword will not pass through your country." Isn't it awesome to know that God knows that you want peace and He wants peace for you too? His peace is a free gift. Remember the words of Leviticus 26:6 the next time fear tries to get you. Remember that God has promised that you will sleep with nothing to fear and He's kicked the monsters out of your closet and from under your bed. The sword will not even pass through your country. Your responsibility is simply to believe His words and trust in Him with your whole heart.

Anchored by Hope

Hebrews 6:19 says, "We have this hope as an anchor for the soul, firm and secure. It enters the inner sanctuary behind the curtain." The inner sanctuary behind the curtain is where God's Spirit dwelled in the Tabernacle. In Old Testament times, only the high priest was allowed in behind the curtain and then, only once a year. The picture this verse from Hebrews paints is that our hope takes us behind the curtain, into the presence of God. That hope is an anchor for our soul. I don't know about you, but my soul could use a little anchoring. Sometimes my emotions get me off course. Sometimes my fear or doubt has me wondering where God is in my life. When a storm hits, an anchor is just what the boat needs to keep it steady. Listen to Hebrews 10:23, "Let us hold unswervingly to the hope we profess, for he who promised is faithful." Take hold of that hope, knowing that the One you're hoping in is faithful to keep you safe and secure.

Love

After Jesus died and rose from the dead, He found some of His disciples fishing one day. He invited them to sit down and eat. So Jesus sat down with Peter by the fire for a fish breakfast, where he asked Peter, "Simon, son of John, do you truly love me more than these?" (John 21:15). Now, Peter's original name was Simon, but Jesus changed it to Peter. However, Simon had gone back to acting like the guy he used to be, not the guy Jesus had called him to be. Peter replied, "Yes Lord, you know that I love you." So Jesus said, "Feed my lambs." This same exchange happened three times. Now, Jesus wasn't worried about His farm here. The lambs He was referring to are the children of God. The food He mentioned is the Word of God. The point Jesus was making was that He wanted Peter doing what He'd called Him to do, which was to serve God. You see, love is an action and something you do. I can say I love my wife, but at some point I need to show her with something I do. You may love your neighbor, but it's not love until you show it. Do you love Jesus? Then show Him.

Be Strong

Ephesians 6:10 says, "Finally, be strong in the Lord, and in His mighty power." This verse lists two places to be strong: in the Lord and in His mighty power. Sometimes we get the idea that being a Christian means being weak or wimpy. The world even says that God is for the weak. But God has a different take on this. He says we are to be strong. Why do we need strength? Because we live in a crazy world with a real enemy. God wants you to be tough! God wants you to win today in your business, your projects, your family, your ministry and your life, and He gives you the tools you need to win. He instructs you to be strong in the Lord and in His mighty power. God's mighty power overcame sin and it raised Christ from the dead. That same power dwells in you. This power makes you strong enough to overcome temptation, trial, or even that unlovable person in your life God wants you to love anyway. You see, in Christ is everything you need to win. Be strong.

Jesus Wept

In John 11, we find Jesus coming to see His good friend Lazarus, who is dead. Now Jesus was not surprised by Lazarus' death. Still, when He got to the grave, it says in John 11:35, "Jesus wept." He didn't just cry, He wept. Sometimes as a Christian, we think everything is supposed to always be perfect and we have to appear like everything is wonderful. You know, we need to look like a squeaky clean Christian with no problems. Here, Jesus gives us a glimpse into His humanity. He felt pain. Listen, if Jesus is allowed to cry, then so are you. Our ability to weep is a gift from God to express our sadness. Jesus expressed His sadness. He wept. But notice, Jesus didn't weep long. He wept to show His sadness, but ultimately, He remained strong in His faith, dried His tears and did the work God had appointed Him to do with great joy. So go ahead and have a good cry. Let it all out. But then dry those tears and get back to the joy of the Lord!

Error

Have you ever got it wrong? I mean, you thought you had it right, but you didn't? We all have lots of opinions and patterns of what we believe about God and life, but the truth is, some of these things are wrong. In Matthew 22:29, Jesus said, "You are in error because you do not know the Scriptures or the power of God." Well, here it is—the key to never being wrong again. We must learn the Scriptures. We must study God's Word. The Bible is the truth, so if our opinion disagrees with the revelation wisdom of God, then we are wrong, and God is right. Notice we must go one step further, though. We also need to know God's power. Many of us may believe in God's power, but do we know it? Knowing His power means taking what we learn from the Scripture, believing God, and then doing it! Jesus said in John 14:12, "Anyone who has faith in me will do what I have been doing." Well, Jesus did some pretty powerful stuff! He saw the supernatural power of God. So can you. So learn it, then believe it, then do it in God's power.

Reputation

Ecclesiastes 7:1 says, "A good name is better than precious ointment" (NKJV). God wants you to have a good name. "A good name" refers to your reputation. Why should God's children have good reputations? Well, think about it, how are you supposed to lead someone to Christ if no one is following you? And how can you be the voice of hope or faith or doing the right thing if no one is listening to you? If you look and smell like the rest of the world, then the world will not know the difference Christ can bring to a life. Proverbs 22:1 says, "A good name is more desirable than great riches." So, having a good name is a big deal. A good name is the reflection of the character and integrity within you. John Maxwell says, "If a good reputation is like gold, then having integrity is like owning the mine." DL Moody wrote, "If I take care of my character, my reputation will take care of itself." So, instead of worrying about your reputation, work on your integrity and the rest will fall into place.

"Would You Like to Supersize that Order?"

The U.S. is one of the most health conscious nations on the planet. We have access to thousands of books on health and nutrition, yet we tend to be the people who sugar and salt our food the most and we'll deep-fry anything. Our serving sizes are big enough to send large animals into hibernation. The problem isn't that we don't know how to be healthy. The problem is that we just like to eat our Twinkies. Fast food is convenient when you're on the go, and we always seem to be going. When we need a pick-me-up, we can caffeinate ourselves until our eyes pop out. First Corinthians 6:19 says, "Do you not know that your body is a temple of the Holy Spirit?" Now, if you recall, God had a very specific design for His temple. It was put together by skilled laborers, using fine fabrics and the finest wood and gold. The temple was well cared for by many attendants. God hand-made your temple—your body. We should care for the temple God has given us. As God's children, let's take care of our temples. Crank up the self-control, get into the right foods and get some exercise.

Generosity

Me, me, me, mine! Sounds like a 2-year-old fighting over toys. Wanting more for ourselves is pretty human, so as a Christian, it is one of the battles we must all grow through. Whether you're two or 92, we like things our way. But God teaches His children to share. Proverbs 22:9 says, "A generous man will himself be blessed, for he shares his food with the poor." God is giving you a big key to being blessed: Be generous. Jesus taught that when a person sues you for your tunic, you should give him your cloak as well. Now, that's generous. You might think that's not fair, but remember, Jesus also taught that whatever you sow, you will reap. If you sow into the poor who cannot repay you, God obviously must step in and repay. Don't make a big deal about your generosity, though. Matthew 6:4 says, "Your Father, who sees what is done in secret, will reward you." Trust God in your obedience and don't worry about what is fair, then God will become your reward, He will become your blessing, and His reward is far more than you can ask, think, or imagine.

Get Yourself to Church

Sunday is here at last—a day of rest! But today feels like a good day to just sleep in. Even Christians may get in the habit of skipping church. Going to church sure feels right, but then again, so does a slow, easy Sunday morning. Acts 20:28 instructs church leaders to, "Be shepherds of the church of God, which he bought with his own blood." Well, how can the leaders shepherd sheep who are not around? When we miss church, we miss out on the opportunity to bring a gift to Jesus by serving and loving the people of God. We miss out on hearing the message of truth and singing to God with our brothers and sisters in the congregation. Church is important. According to this scripture, the church was bought with Christ's blood. That is a steep price to pay to build something. The church is important to Christ. He needs you there. Maybe it's an issue of discipline for you; you just can't seem to make yourself go. A great way to enforce the discipline of church attendance is to volunteer to serve at your church. Then you will be obligated to go because you have something to do, and then everyone wins!

Love: The Most Important Gift

Jesus said in Matthew 5:23-24 that if you are giving to God then suddenly remember your brother is upset with you, you should leave your gift and go be reconciled to your brother. Then, you can come back and give. In Malachi 2:13-14, we find God is not pleased with the gifts of the people and the reason he states is this: "The LORD is acting as the witness between you and the wife of your youth, because you have broken faith with her." In both of these passages, we see our gifts to God are affected by our relationships, both with our brothers and sisters in the Lord and with our spouse. God is telling us it is important that we get along with each other. He's saying that we show our love for Him when we love others. First John 4:20 says it like this, "Anyone who does not love his brother whom he has seen, cannot love God, whom he has not seen." God wants us all to get along. Love your neighbor, love your brother, love your spouse and in this way, you are showing love to God and your gift to Him is like that of Abel who loved, and not of Cain, who did not love.

Watch What You Say

The story of Job strikes fear into the hearts of many people. In Job 1:11, Satan tells God, "Stretch out your hand and strike everything he (Job) has, and he will surely curse you to your face." Now God didn't stretch out His hand and do any striking, in case you are wondering. He gave Satan the permission to do what Satan does—destroy things. Don't miss the point of Job's story by going into fear that the same things are going to happen to you. Remember that Jesus died on the cross and changed everything. Job didn't have a Redeemer like we do! All the stories you read in the Old Testament must be washed through the cross. You are highly favored, blessed and well protected as the righteous of the Lord. Now that we've cleared up that confusion, notice what Satan's goal was. His goal was to change how Job spoke about God. His goal was to get Job to curse God. What we speak is so very important. God created the heavens and earth with words. When Zechariah spoke doubt out loud about the coming of John the Baptist, the angel closed his mouth and he could not speak until the baby was born. So, what are you saying? How do you describe God? Are you describing your mess, or are you speaking what God says? Choose your words wisely.

The Good Fight

In 1 Timothy 6:12, Paul tells Timothy to "Fight the good fight of the faith." We like a good fight whether it be boxing, wrestling, or the fight at school everyone runs to watch. If you like a good fight, God has good news for you. He tells you to fight the good fight. If there is a good fight, that means there must also be bad fights. What's an example of a bad fight? A fight with your boss is a bad fight because even if you win, you lose. Listen up teenagers: fighting with your parents is never a good idea because even if you win, you lose. What if you eliminated all the fighting in your life except for the fights God asks you to take on? You would certainly be more rested up for the good fight, and you would probably get yourself in less trouble. What if you just said to yourself, *You know what, I'm not gonna fight bad fights ever again.* That leaves you to only fight the good fight of the faith. This fight will keep you believing God. When things aren't perfect, you may be tempted to doubt God. Don't! Fight doubt, keep the faith, and hold unswervingly to the hope you profess, because God is faithful.

What You Say About Others

Do you ever say, "Oh that guy? Yeah, I don't like him"? Have you ever said, "There's something wrong with her"? We open our mouths and say stuff we shouldn't say all the time. So what's the problem? James 3:8-10 says, "No man can tame the tongue... with the tongue we praise our Lord and Father, and with it we curse men, who have been made in God's likeness... this should not be." Notice the reminder that we're all made in God's likeness. So when we speak against man, we are speaking against God who created him. When the people of Israel grumbled against Moses, in reality they were not grumbling against Moses, but against God. We can speak against sin, doubt, and the bad things of the world. There's lots of stuff we can disagree with, but we should not speak against people themselves. If you are cursing others, then you are joining the wrong team. Bless others, walk in love and forgiveness, understand others, and never forget that you sometimes fail, too.

Resisting Temptation

Jesus came and took our sins away. Isn't that wonderful? No more worrying about our sin, right? Well, it's true that when you trust Jesus as your Lord and Savior, you are forgiven, but when we sin, there are consequences. What do I mean? Well, if you break the laws of the land, like speeding, you can ask God to forgive you, but you may still get a ticket. A Christian husband can be forgiven of indiscretions, but he may still lose all that he's built because of one slip into temptation. So sin is still to be avoided greatly if don't want to face consequences. I haven't met a follower of Christ who wasn't trying to avoid sin. We are trying, but we still fall and then the world gets all excited and points out our failures. Hebrews 12:4 says, "In your struggle against sin, you have not yet resisted to the point of shedding your blood." When Jesus was in the Garden of Gethsemane, He sweat blood as He obeyed God. This is a struggle. My point is this, when it comes to resisting temptation, you can always try harder. Ask God for the strength to obey, to overcome, to love, to give, and to be holy.

Don't Be Lazy

Hebrews 6:12 says, "We do not want you to become lazy, but to imitate those who through faith and patience inherit what has been promised." It ain't just your momma who's on you to stop being lazy... God doesn't want you to be lazy either. If you look around, there is a lot to be done like expand the church, fund the missionaries, get the message of Christ on the media airways, and get love into the hearts of people. The key to accomplishing it all—not being lazy. We must imitate those who through faith and patience, inherit what has been promised. Those who choose to not have faith or those who refuse to wait with patience are considered lazy, and the lazy will not inherit the promise. Do you need more faith? Well, faith comes by hearing the Word of God, so get more Word into you. Patience is the end result of learning to not give up when things don't happen right away. Abraham waited 25 years for his promise to arrive. How long can you keep believing while you wait? Hey now, no quitting and no being lazy!

Who Are You Following?

In Luke 6:39, Jesus asked the question, "Can a blind man lead a blind man?" Ultimately, Jesus wasn't talking about people who are physically blind; He was talking about those who have no idea where to go in life. When you don't know where to go, you stumble through the darkness of life and probably will stub your toe something terrible. So, who is leading you? The people we hang out with influence our lives, no question. Some of that influence may be bad. Psalm 61:2 says "Lead me to the rock that is higher than I". God wants to be your leader. He will lead you to somewhere better than where you are. He is leading you to the rock. It's higher and it's not necessarily an easy journey to get there. The journey might take some effort and there may be a wilderness to cross. You may even wonder sometimes if it's the right way, but if you are following God, you can know it is always the right way.

The End

Lately, there's been a lot of talk about the end of the world. It's on the movies and TV. I even saw a billboard stating the date the end of the world it is going to happen. Well, if you're reading this, then that must mean we are all still here. Sometimes people ask me if I'm worried about the coming of the end of the world. The truth is, no, I'm not. Do you want to know why? It's because I've read the back of the Book a few times now, and I know who wins. God wins. And remember, if God wins, we win. So what should we do? Second Peter 3:11-12 says, "You ought to live holy and godly lives as you look forward to the day of God and speed its coming." There are some keys here for us. First, we should live holy and godly lives. That's not easy, but God wouldn't ask us to do something unless we could do it with His help, right? Next, God tells us we should look forward to the day. Yeah, that's right. We should not be afraid of it, but be excited about it. Now if you don't know God, you should dread that day. But it's not too late to know Him. Say out loud, "Jesus is Lord," believe He died and rose again, ask God for forgiveness, and fear no more!

This One's for Mom

The month of May brings Mother's Day. My dad asked me once, "Hey, how much money did you spend on your girlfriend's birthday?" I replied, "$60." Then he asked, "Great. So what are you going to buy your mom for Mom's day?" *Uh oh.* That girlfriend is long gone now, but my mom, well, she's still my mom. One of the Ten Commandments instructs us to honor Mom. Whether you're a kid or an adult, whether your mom was perfect or not so perfect, or maybe even never around, you have a responsibility as a Christian to honor your mom. So plan something great for her, call her, make her something special, or buy her the moon. Think about what you could do or say that would make her feel valuable. You may need to start by searching your own heart to forgive her, or maybe you need to ask her to forgive you. Whatever the case, let this be a Mother's Day to remember and one full of honor. Just think, without her, well, where would you be?

To Be Happy

What is it going to take to make you happy? A person who has nothing might say, "I just need some food and a billion dollars, then I'll be happy." A person who is sick might say, "Health will make me happy." Now, God will meet your needs, and Jesus certainly came to heal the sick, but remember there are plenty of healthy, rich people who are not happy. It seems like we all just need one more thing to be happy. *If I just make the cheer squad, I'll be happy. When I finally get married, I'll be happy. When I win the lottery, I'll be happy.* Psalm 4:7 says, "You have filled my heart with greater joy than when their grain and new wine abound." Real joy, joy that lasts, comes from the Lord. This doesn't mean God doesn't want you to have blessings or health. It just means you shouldn't rely on anything but God for happiness. He gives joy, and it has nothing to do with what you need. "Happy" is something you can be right now. Let God fill your heart with joy, and you'll be smiling more than the people who seemingly have everything, because happiness comes from God.

Good Tests vs. Bad Tests

Matthew 4 tells us that Satan took Jesus up to highest point of the temple and said, "Hey, jump off and the angels will catch You." Jesus responded, saying, "It is also written: 'Do not put the Lord your God to the test'" (v. 7). Okay, I get it—no testing God. But then God is talking about giving Him ten percent of our income as a tithe and in Malachi 3:10, He says, "Test me in this…and see if I will not throw open the floodgates of heaven and pour out so much blessing that you will not have room enough for it." So in one scripture, it says don't put God to the test, and then in a different one, God tells us to test Him. So, which is it? You can test God when it comes to His principals like tithing. He is saying, "Trust Me with your money, give Me your heart. See if I won't keep my word." But, there are tests that are wrong. Testing God for sport, just to see if He's paying attention or if He's really as strong as He says He is, that's wrong. These tests reveal that you doubt God, and Satan wants nothing more than for you to doubt God.

Get the Doubt Out

God had promised Abraham 25 years earlier that he would have child, but at the age of 99, he still did not have that promised child. I'm sure many of Abraham's friends and acquaintances had no problem having children, even though some of them may have not even known or believed in God. Yet, Abraham still had no child, though he really desired one. Most people, after 25 years, would be pretty doubtful that the promise would be kept. Abraham, however, did not doubt. Romans 4:20 says that Abraham, "Did not waver through unbelief regarding the promise of God, but was strengthened in his faith." The very next year, at the age of 100, Abraham and Sarah had the promised child. Jesus told us in Matthew 21:21, if you have faith and do not doubt, you can speak to mountains and have them move. We don't need a lot of faith, just faith the size of a mustard seed, but we must have no doubt. When we begin to doubt even just a little part of God or His Word, we are wavering in doubt and that hinders our miracle. If you are in need of a miracle, stand strong on what God said! God said it, so it's true. Believe and not doubt!

Real Bread

I was tempted greatly the other day by a wonderful moist piece of warm cake filled with hot fudge and topped with ice cream. That cursed dessert called out to me from the pit to indulge and eat. Well now, not eating dessert isn't quite in the Ten Commandments, so I caved. I'm an easy target. But Jesus, after not eating for forty days, was approached by Satan. Satan tempted Jesus to turn some rocks into bread and eat them. Jesus' response was this, "Man does not live on bread alone, but on every word that comes from the mouth of God." God's Word is what gives us life. This is not the same life we get from chocolate cake, or even bread, instead it is life that lasts eternally. It's real life. We can be ALIVE with the hope, joy, peace, patience, and love that comes from God's bread. And like we eat every day, we need God's bread every single day, not just on Sundays. The Bible promises that meditating on God's Word will cause everything we touch to prosper. Are we reading the Bible enough? Are we getting that bread? Set aside a time for God. Take notes on what you are learning from God's Word. Really eat it. Chew it up. What do you want to learn about?

Our Passover Lamb

Why did Jesus have to die for us? God told Adam that if he ate of the tree of the Knowledge of Good and Evil, that he would surely die. As you know, Adam ate and sinned. Now, when Adam ate, you were in Adam, so when you were born into this world, you were born a sinner. Sin passes through the man. But, Jesus was not born of man. Mary was a virgin and yet was found with child. Jesus was the first man since Adam to come into the world sinless. Jesus, however, remained sinless, completely innocent. Now, remember that God had promised that Adam would surely die if he disobeyed God. In His mercy, God allowed a substitute to die in man's place. An animal could be sacrificed in place of man to atone for sin. Blood had to be shed. When the Israelites were leaving Egypt, they sacrificed a lamb without blemish and painted the blood over their doorposts as protection from the angel of death. That lamb was dying to atone for sin. This was called the Passover feast, and it is celebrated every year on the 14th day of the first month of the Hebrew Calendar. This is, in fact, the same day Jesus was crucified, 1500 years later, on the 14th day of the first month, at the Passover celebration. He is the Lamb of God. He is the Lamb without blemish that was sacrificed for us. When God told Adam that if he sinned he would surely die, someone had to pay that price. Jesus paid it for all man and for all time. Jesus is the Lamb of God. Thank you, Jesus!

Influence for the Kingdom

Selfish ambition is bad, but ambition for God's glory is good. In Genesis 12, God promised to make your name great. Why would He want your name to be great? Because God wants His people to have a voice on this planet. Isaiah 61:3 says that Christ will, "provide for those who grieve in Zion, to bestow on them a crown of beauty instead of ashes." "Those who grieve in Zion" is referring to those who have received Christ and entered the Kingdom of God, but are not okay with the how the world currently is. Those who grieve in Zion would like to see things get better. We look at this world and see hunger, disease, poverty, wrong influences in entertainment and education, corrupt government systems, and greed, and we want things to improve. If you have ambitions to help make a positive change in this world for God, then Jesus has a crown of beauty for you. Why a crown? A crown says that you are in charge. Jesus is the King of kings, and He is crowning you with a crown of beauty. He gives you a crown of beauty because He wants others to follow you because they are attracted to you and they like you. Sometimes, Christians don't realize that Christ wants us to be influencing the world as salt and light. Leadership is influence.

Light a Fire

In Isaiah 61:3, God promises to give us the oil of gladness instead of mourning. So, what is this oil of gladness? Oil in the Bible is symbolic of the anointing, which is God's supernaturally empowered purpose for your life. (Try saying that three times fast.) For instance, David was anointed by Samuel to be king when he was just a shepherd boy. The anointing was for his purpose. Oil was also used as fuel in lamps to produce fire, which gave light. So the oil of gladness is God's fuel for the fire within you, which enables you to accomplish the plan He has for your life and your purpose. The oil is the supernatural power provided by the Spirit of God within you to help drive you to that purpose. Notice, it is the oil of *gladness*. We could all use a little more gladness as we carry out our purpose. What has God anointed you to do? To help you discover your purpose, ask yourself what lights your fire. God knows we will need a great deal of fuel to stay motivated through all of the battles along the way of reaching His plan for our life. The oil of gladness within you should provide plenty of light and passion to get you well on your way to fulfilling your God-given purpose.

The Ghost Within

In John 14:17, Jesus was telling the disciples that He was going to be leaving, but He would send the Holy Spirit. He goes on to say, "You know him, for he lives with you, and will be in you." Man could not receive the Holy Spirit inside until Jesus had completed His work. After Jesus died and resurrected, He breathed on the disciples and said, "Receive the Holy Spirit." In Acts 2, we see the account of when they were all filled with the Holy Spirit. This is important stuff. The Spirit that lived in Jesus now lives in you. That is, the Spirit of God. The Spirit that used to live in the Ark of the Covenant that was in the temple now lives in you. You are now the temple of the Holy Spirit. Jesus could heal the sick and walk on water, but He said you would do even greater things. Now, I know some don't like talking about the Holy Spirit living in you. But, I can't ignore what God says. The Bible says when I receive Christ, I receive the Spirit of God within me and I'm good with that. Jesus said the Spirit will lead me to truth and remind me of things that Jesus said. Well, I could use some leading and reminding from time to time. Plus, the Spirit brings with Him His gifts and fruit. And who wouldn't want gifts and fruit?

A Weak Offense

Has anyone ever done something or said something that offended you? What are we supposed to do with that? Proverbs 19:11 says, "A man's wisdom gives him patience; it is to his glory to overlook an offense." When we get offended, it really has the power to mess up our emotions and our day. It can even mess up a relationship. But what if you misunderstood the situation? Have you ever said something that someone else took the wrong way? If we choose to not be offended and instead, choose to love and see the good in others, then we are exercising wise patience. Your life is full of people who are human, and humans will make mistakes. Anyone can get mad, that's easy. Jesus isn't asking us to take the easy road. The promise is that when you choose to overlook an offense and not get offended, it will be to your glory.

Rich in Every Way

In 2 Corinthians 9, Paul tells us that God loves a cheerful giver. Then he goes on to say that as we give, God will increase our store of seed and "you will be made rich in every way so that you can be generous on every occasion" (v. 11). We really will reap when we sow. Sowing more seed means a bigger harvest. When we give cheerfully, we activate this promise of God. He will make you rich in every way. "Every way" is an important phrase. God isn't just making us rich financially so that we can continue in our giving. He is also making us rich spiritually and rich in love and health. Now this doesn't mean you just put your feet up and wait for the magic gold brick to show up in your mailbox. You have to put your hands to work so God has something to bless. The promise is that as you give to the Lord, God will begin to increase every area of your life. If your life is in need of increase, try sowing more seed. Then when the harvest comes, you can be generous on every occasion.

Keep Moving

In Exodus, we find the Israelites following God out of Egypt, right up to the edge of the Promised Land, but then they stopped. They would not follow God in. They saw the people living in the land that they would need to fight and they got scared. I wonder how many times we have been following the Lord and then we got to an opportunity that looked a bit risky and we hesitated? It was a scary proposition, going in to the Promised Land and fighting. When we arrive at something we think we can't do, maybe instead of turning back we should close our eyes, grit our teeth, and keep going, because we know our Lord is with us. That's one of His names you know, Immanuel, which means God with us. Forty years later when Joshua led the people into the Promised Land, they had to step into the Jordan River while it was flooding. This took guts. It wasn't until they stepped in that the water stopped flowing and they crossed over. I know things get tricky in life, but maybe instead of hesitating, maybe it is time to keep moving and step into the river. Now take another step. God is with you and He's really strong.

Fully Charged

In the middle of a phone call, my phone battery went dead. For the rest of the day, my phone would not function until I put it on the charger when I got home. Then it came back on. Sometimes, I'm like that phone. I feel like my batteries are running low and I need to recharge. You hear people say, "Oh I can't wait till Friday night." Why? Because it's when our weekend starts. We can rest and recharge for the next week. But, how do you recharge? Luke 5:16 says that Jesus often withdrew to lonely places and prayed. Jesus was always giving of Himself teaching and praying for others, but Jesus was living in a human body and He would have needed some recharge time. Jesus charged up His batteries by getting away with God. How do you recharge? Is it by watching TV or partying all weekend? Partying is not a good charger. If you want a full charge, try a little God time. Pray and spend time with your Savior. Get on that charger.

To See or Not to See

Jesus said in Matthew 6:5, "And when you pray, do not be like the hypocrites, for they love to pray standing in the synagogues and on the street corners to be seen by men." What was wrong with the prayer of these men? Was it that people saw them praying? Or, was it the fact that they *wanted* people to see them? *Ding Ding* – it was that they wanted people to see them. They wanted to be seen by men as super holy or something. They prayed on the street corners to look good. Now, Daniel prayed in his window facing the city and all could see him. Was this wrong? NO! Daniel prayed as he did to be a light, to influence others, and to let the whole world know that He was a praying man regardless of the social and political climate. Jesus is telling us that God is concerned with why we do things. If we do them so that others will think we are super spiritual, then He regards us as hypocrites. If you're wondering where you stand, a good thing to do is to go in your closed room and pray and allow God to search your heart and align your intentions. Jesus prayed in the open often, but He did it for the right reasons!

What Are You Wearing Today?

"Is that what you're wearing today? Really?" Now that sounds like something your parents might ask or for me, it sounds like what my wife says to me almost every day. But, today it's not your parents asking, and it's not even me asking. Instead, it's God asking you what you are wearing. In Colossians 3:12, God asks that His people clothe themselves with kindness. He wants us to put on kindness and wear it. You see, when you put something on, then it's all over you. It's what people see when they see you and it becomes a way of describing you—like "the guy in the yellow hat." Wearing kindness is great. You can wear it at the beach or in the snow. It seems to go with everything and when you have it on no one is going to say to you, "I can't believe you're wearing kindness with those jeans." Kindness is always clean and freshly pressed and there is no need to take it off once you have it on. Try on some kindness today. You'll find yourself being nice to others, seeing good in others, helping, caring, and wanting others to win. You'll find yourself being encouraging, smiling, and for once in your life, finally matching. Let's all put on some kindness today and show the world a little Jesus in us.

Rogue Self

The Word teaches that you are a spirit, but you have a self. It's yours. It is yourself. Jesus taught in Matthew 16 that you need to learn to deny yourself. Sometimes self wants things you don't need or shouldn't have. It may want to sleep all day, or eat the wrong things, or get all emotional and say stuff that gets you in trouble. But God has given us an out. Here's the solution for a rogue self. You ready? One of the fruit of the Spirit is self-control. It's a fruit because it grows over time. Proverbs 25:28 says, "Like a city whose walls are broken down is a man who lacks self-control." If you are city with no walls, you have no defense from attacks. And in this world, I can tell you that we need some good defense. So how can we grow our self-control? Well, Jesus went into the wilderness and didn't eat for 40 days. He was telling His body who was boss. Now I'm not telling you to stop eating, but I'm encouraging us all to exercise our self-control so it can grow. Build it up so you can have nice strong walls around your city.

Who Are You Going to Believe?

In the Garden of Eden, the snake was talking to Eve. Now, if you ever run into a snake trying to sell you fruit, well, don't buy from him. The serpent started by saying, "Did God really say...?" The serpent was trying to paint a different picture of who God is. He was telling Eve stuff about God that made God look like He was holding back on her. Satan wants us to believe lies about God and to change who we think God is. Satan is still doing this today. He has much of the world believing things about God that aren't true. Now our belief does not change what is true, but it can change our personal reality. For instance, a person can decide to believe that there is no God. Their belief doesn't change the truth, but it does change that person's reality, and they will live a life without God. When I hear personalities on TV try and describe who they think God is, it is never my God they are describing. As a Christian, we have a responsibility to get to know God for ourselves. Let God tell us who He is, which He does in the Bible. So get into the Bible and study it, and find God's truths. Find out who God says He is.

You Too

Have you ever had someone let you down like a friend, a brother or sister, mom or dad, even a hero or spiritual leader? Have you ever had someone in your life hurt you or break faith or trust? Well, if you haven't, you are a rare case. People let you down. But remember this, YOU have let others down too. It says in John 2:24, "But Jesus would not entrust himself to them, for he knew all men." He knew what was in a man. You see, Jesus knows that we are built out of dirt and that we have weaknesses. He knows that there is a tempter. Jesus loved us and gave His all for us, but He also understood us and gave us grace for our weakness. Understanding and grace is what we need to gain for others. When someone else lets you down, don't let it divide you from them. Instead, apply understanding and grace. Hey, you mess up too! Only Christ gets it all perfect. Pray for those who stumble, walk in forgiveness and love. Don't be so surprised when a human makes a mistake. Instead of being the one who feels so let down, be the one who helps lift others back up. That way when you fall, someone will be quick to help you back on your feet.

On Time

As followers of Christ, we are trying to do the right thing, but we find out pretty quickly that it isn't so easy. It's a tough world. Our flesh likes stuff it shouldn't. Our friends aren't always super helpful in our quest to live right and there is a tempter, the devil. So how about just a simple thing like being on time? You know that Jesus showed up in Jerusalem at the exact right time and went into the Garden of Gethsemane to pray when the time was right. He was crucified on the night of preparation. As our Passover Lamb, it was so important that He got the timing perfect. Now, sometimes we are late for stuff. In some cases it really doesn't matter, but sometimes it really does. Sometimes people are counting on you and even waiting for you. When someone has to wait for you, you have stolen something from them: time. Now I'm late too, so I say we work on this together. If you are late for work, you know it really isn't traffic's fault, or the fault of your alarm clock. Wake up earlier, leave earlier, give yourself enough time so that if there is a problem, you'll still be on time. It's a simple thing like being on time that can sometimes be the exact right thing to do.

Toast

I am a big fan of toast. I don't mean clinking glasses together. I'm talking about dropping a piece of bread in the toaster, then buttering it and maybe even adding jelly or honey. I mix it up. Toast is great for what time of day? Well, breakfast. But there is a better and even more important kind of toast to eat for breakfast. While Jesus was fasting, Satan tried to get Jesus to turn some stones into toast, well, bread actually (toasters hadn't been invented yet). So Jesus said, "Man does not live on bread alone, but on every word that comes from the mouth of God" (Matthew 4:4). Now, we have access to something so valuable and important—the Bible, which is the word of God. It is the true wisdom of God and it gives us the opportunity to read and fathom mysteries and to hear God speak. We can do all this every morning, just by reading the Bible. This is the best toast of all and it is never burnt, soggy or dry, and it is always exactly what I need. So, get up tomorrow a bit earlier and have some Word of God toast with your toast. It's like a cinnamon Pop Tart of love for your soul, manna for the man of God, 7-grain wholesome heart healthy food to keep you going all day.

French Fries and Diamonds

What's the difference between a french fry and a diamond? I mean, both are wonderful and both are desirable. People like french fries and people like diamonds. The difference is the value. A french fry is common, easy to find, and inexpensive. It comes in a paper box with other fries. A diamond is held behind a glass case; it is beautiful and rare. It comes exquisitely wrapped. Okay girls, this is a lesson for you. God created you as a diamond, a rare and unique beautiful creature; a true gift from God. But you can choose to be that diamond, rare and valuable, or you can choose to be a french fry. Now, when it comes to the boys, french fries may get a lot of attention, but in the end the boys don't place much value on a french fry. Boys like french fries, but a french fry is not something to be saved. The right kind of boys aren't even into french fries. They aren't interested in common, mediocre, or just average. The right man is looking for the diamond that is rare and still in the glass case. A diamond doesn't just wear anything and doesn't just act the way other girls do. Don't be a french fry, be a diamond. In the end, diamonds win.

Stripped

Joseph had a dream at the age of 17 that he would be a leader. Joseph's brothers didn't like him and they surely didn't like his dream. Genesis 37:23-24 says that Joseph's brothers stripped him of his robe and then they threw him into a cistern. Later, they sold him into slavery. This began Joseph's journey towards his dream. One day, he would be second in command of all the land, but not today. The robe the brothers stripped off Joseph was the robe his dad had made for him. The robe represented the fact that he was his father's most loved son. But it also was a reason his brothers hated him. In order to get going on toward his destiny, Joseph had to be stripped of what everyone else thought about him—which was what the robe represented—because it just didn't matter. Once the brothers stripped the robe from Joseph, they then dipped it in blood. This represents the truth that the outer garment that is trying to define you needs to be crucified with Christ. Joseph had to find out who God created him to be. You see, we often wear around what others have put on us, like insecurities and strengths that come from man. But God wishes us to be rid of this garment so we can run our race. It just doesn't matter what others think about you, it matters what God thinks.

Impossible? Good!

Joseph had a God given dream that one day he would lead, which might have seemed attainable to him since he was the favorite son. But the dream started to look impossible when Joseph's brothers sold him into slavery. As a slave, he expected never to see his family again as he would seemingly be a slave forever. Later, he was thrown in prison, which, in his mind, took him even further from the dream God had given him. For nine years, Joseph was a slave and then he spent another four years in prison. I imagine he wondered how this dream would ever come to pass. Have you ever had a dream? God gives us dreams to get us thinking, praying, and trying to head in a direction that He has for us. But not everyone realizes their dreams. Does the dream in your heart seem impossible now? Well good, because the dream must become impossible to have life. You see, Joseph's dream needed to become impossible. If he could have made his dream a reality on his own, then how would God receive glory? It is when our dreams seem most impossible that God has the most power. After 13 years of having a dream that seemed impossible, Joseph's dream came to pass and he was placed second in command of all the land. Does your dream seem hopeless? Well, get ready!

Diligence

Well, I'm still talking about Joseph and his dream. So far, we've talked about becoming who God says we are and that our dream needs to become impossible so that God is employed to help bring it to reality. Joseph, both as a slave and in prison, shows us something about his character. He was not a man who felt beaten. His dream that God had given him of becoming a ruler must have still been in his heart as something God would accomplish. He could have quit on life, feeling like his family and even God had quit on him. Instead, Joseph was diligent as a slave and as a prisoner. He experienced promotion in both areas because of his diligence. Having diligence even when things seem bleak is a key to realizing your God given dreams. Romans 5:3-5 says, "We also rejoice in our sufferings, because we know that suffering produces perseverance; perseverance, character; and character, hope, and hope does not disappoint us." Was Joseph suffering? Well yes, a bit, but by remaining diligent, he produced character and hope. Joseph worked hard for nothing, and then God became his reward as his dream was realized. God gives us this story for you and your dreams to hear. Stay diligent. For Joseph, it only took 13 years of diligence. On the 14 the year, the dream became reality!

Be a Dream Helper

Are we still on Joseph? Well, yes. We continue to look at what it takes to have your God-given dreams come true as we look at Joseph and his dreams. So far, we've learned to take off our manmade robe and be who God made us to be. We learned that we can't quit when our dream seems impossible, but we must remain diligent, giving God the chance to move on our behalf. Today, we continue with Joseph's story. The king's baker and cupbearer had both been thrown into prison, where Joseph was. It says in Genesis 40 that Joseph noticed one day that they were sad so he asked them what was wrong. Well, they had both had dreams and didn't know what the dreams meant. Joseph helped them understand their dreams. This act of helping his fellow inmates was a key to Joseph's dream becoming reality because two years later, Pharoah would have a dream that needed interpreting and the cupbearer would remember that Joseph could help. The point is that for our dreams to come true, we need to be willing to stop and help others with their dreams. Joseph cared that these men seemed down. A dream by its very nature is selfish. A lot of people, while chasing a dream, run over other people. This is not God's plan. Care for others. Help others win and they will help you win.

Thank You, Sir. May I Have Another?

Hey kids, isn't being disciplined fun? Well, okay, no. I couldn't wait to get older so that I wouldn't have to endure discipline anymore. But then I got married, and went to work, and I serve God. So I have a surprise for you... discipline keeps happening. Whether it's the wife, the boss, or God, we still get disciplined. Everyone gets disciplined. The question is, how do you react to discipline? Anyone can get mad when being disciplined and anyone can argue or pout about it. That is a normal reaction, but a person who wins in life is one who receives correction well. Receiving correction is harder to do. It means admitting you're wrong. Sometimes you admit you're wrong even when you don't think you're wrong. It means taking a look at yourself and asking how you can be better or how you can change and grow through the discipline. Hebrews 12:11 says, "No discipline seems pleasant at the time, but painful. Later on, however it produces a harvest of righteousness and peace for those who have been trained by it." The next time you are disciplined, remember that you are about to get better and get some peace about the process.

The Right Bloodline

A thoroughbred horse is a horse that has been bred to win. Often referred to as being hot blooded, it is the bloodline of these horses that is the primary focus. Having the right blood means having the speed, lightness, and endurance to win. For this reason, horse breeding has been an art since the 17th century with an emphasis on using the strongest and fastest horses to bring about the next generation. Now, what does this mean for you today? Well, you are created to win and when you received Christ, you received His blood. Now a brother of Christ and joint heir of the Lord's inheritance, you are a child of God. You are created to win and you have the blood to win. You see, the right blood—Christ's blood—means you have the mind of Christ and the righteousness of God. You have the Spirit of God in you, the ability to move mountains, the sword of the spirit, the shield of faith, the helmet of salvation, the belt of truth, feet fitted with the readiness that comes from the gospel of peace, eternal life and you are armed for battle. To God be all glory and power! Christ loves us and has freed us from our sins by His blood. You can't lose! Ready, set, go!

The Master Decoder

In 1 Corinthians 2:9 Paul is quoting Isaiah saying, "No eye has seen, no ear has heard, no mind has conceived what God has prepared for those who love him." Then Paul writes in verse 10, "But God has revealed it to us by his Spirit." You see, until Christ came, what Isaiah said was true. No one could know this manifold hidden wisdom of God. It was like a secret. But then Paul says, "but we know." Why? Because Jesus changed *everything*. God has now revealed these things by His Spirit. Are there secret things of God? Yes! Okay, so how do we find out what these secrets are? Paul goes on to say in verses 10-12 that only God's Spirit knows God's thoughts and now that we have access to that Spirit, we can know His thoughts. This is a great gift. God has given us the decoder ring to the hidden mysteries in His Word, and it is the Spirit. If you want to know what God thinks about something, you can just ask and then listen to the Spirit of God. Go ahead, ask Him if He thinks you should give an offering or ask Him if he thinks you should go to church. Ask Him what He thinks you should do, then do it. Then you win!

Sing-a-Long

Every time I go to church, there are all these people singing. What is this? Can I wait till the music is over to come in? When is the preacher going to start? What songs are these? You know, I think our culture sometimes misses out on praise and worship. Imagine the shepherd boy, David, out with the sheep, singing songs to the Lord when Samuel arrived to anoint him to be king. Before he took the throne and even after, David wrote over a hundred songs that are now in the Bible. In 2 Samuel 23:1 it says, "These are the last words of David." Okay, so in his dying breath, what did David say? (This is going to be a profound moment.) His last words were a song. A man who lived his destiny, became king as God called him to, and a man after God's own heart—his last words were a song! David started his life with worshipping God and ended it the same way. His life was like a praise and worship sandwich with cheese. The next time you walk into church while the music's playing, jump in like David. Learn to worship God in song like David. You might as well start singing now, since it just keeps going when you get to heaven!

Qualified

In many races, there is a qualifying round. The qualifying round determines whether you are qualified to run in the big race for the prize. Getting a new job can be like running a qualifying race. It is tough to be hired if they find you to be unqualified. Worse yet, certain things can disqualify you from being able to participate at all. Thus, no prize for you. Did you know though, that in Christ, you have been qualified for the prize? Colossians 1:12 says we are, "...giving thanks to the Father, who has qualified you to share in the inheritance of the saints in the kingdom of light." So there is an inheritance, and you get to share in it. And, I'm sure it is good. Are you qualified because you ran a good preliminary round or went to the right school? Are you qualified because you have the skill, or a proven record, or the right friends, or the right car? Or because you have no tattoos? Nope. God has qualified you, and it's free. You are qualified because Jesus ran the qualifying round on your behalf, and when you receive Him, His run becomes your run. The prize is yours and the inheritance is free. Jesus won it all.

Decisions, Decisions

Deuteronomy 30:19 says, "I have set before you life and death, blessings and curses. Now choose life." Choices, choices, choices. Donuts or broccoli, cheesecake or asparagus? Funny how the stuff that tastes the worst is the stuff we are supposed to eat. The stuff that we want right now, well it's not that good for us. If we go with the fruits, veggies and the good foods, it may not be that great right now, but we will live longer healthier lives. Life is full of similar decisions concerning things that I can do right now that might feel good, but in the long run they'll leave me in a mess. For instance, I may decide to buy a bunch of stuff that I cannot afford by using my credit card. Or maybe a relationship with a girlfriend is getting physical fast. Either of these things may feel good now, but they'll trip me up in the long run. It's easier to watch TV than read the Bible. It's easier to complain then to pray. And it's not always easy to give an offering. God's ways often take longer to produce results and they take discipline, but in the end God's way leaves me with a healthier and happier life. So when it comes to your health, your relationships, your faith, or your money—when it comes to making a choice—don't take the easy road. Take the godly road.

Don't Spend, Sow

How do you spend your time? Anything we spend is gone. Like when we spend money, once spent, that money is gone. God teaches us to sow. He teaches us by example, as He sows into our lives. Sowing produces; spending wastes. To gain more, we must plant. We must learn to sow and we must learn to invest. So instead of thinking of spending time, think of investing time. Don't spend time with your family. Instead, invest time into your family. It's a mental switch. If I'm investing time, then I'm not distracted. I'm not texting or surfing the web or playing my favorite phone game; I can put myself in a position of sowing, of uplifting, of encouraging, and of giving. With my family, I try to create good memories. When you're off to work, don't spend time at the job. Instead, invest time into the job, because then you can expect a return. Anyone can show up to work and go through the motions. Instead, put your heart into it. Be excellent, be diligent and make an investment out of it. Give more than you are receiving. Work more than you are paid for. Be it relationships, your occupation, or whatever, sow everywhere you go. Plant, and make life an investment. Give more than you get. God is your reward.

Old vs. New

The Old Testament makes up the majority of the Bible and the information there is so important. But then there is a New Testament. Why is there a New Testament? Well, think about what is in the New Testament—the account of the birth, death, and resurrection of Jesus. His coming to earth was prophesied and when this happened, a New Testament was created. "New" indicates that something has changed. What changed? Well, everything. I am explaining this because it is important to realize that when Jesus came to earth, died, and rose again, the relationship between man and God changed. It is different now than it was in the Old Testament because of the blood of Jesus. Hebrews 9:15 says that, "He has died as a ransom to set them free from the sins committed under the first covenant." Who is free? You are, if you have trusted Jesus as your Savior. The Old Testament is the story of man who kept failing, falling, and suffered punishment. The New Testament tells the story of a Man who lived perfectly righteous, and yet was crucified, so that all who believe would be seen as righteous by God. What changed? Well, Christ brought grace and forgiveness. He brought freedom, healing, and His Spirit. Everything has changed. As you read the Old Testament, always view it through the story of Christ and think about how our relationship with our Creator is different now then it was then.

We Win

My brother TiVos sports on Sundays. Since we are typically minister-ing all day, we miss the big games. So, he goes back and watches them after the game is over. One day, he started to watch a particularly important football game, already knowing from seeing the news that his team had won the game. In the first quarter, his team fell behind. They had an interception and then a fumble. Even into the fourth quarter, his team was losing. Still, he was never afraid or even stressed. Why? Well, he already knew who the winner would be. He knew that somehow his team was going to win. He didn't know how, but he did know for a fact that they would win. This is like our Christianity. Sometimes we find ourselves in the pit and in a mess. Sometimes we find ourselves in a storm and we sweat and stress, but really, if we read the end of the Book, we know that we win. We may not know how God is going to pull it out, but we put our trust in Him. Don't give space for doubt and fear. Instead, stand firm knowing that God is bigger. He's on your team, and He will win the war. Though setbacks come and things look bleak, always have faith and fear not. God is your shield and your exceedingly great reward.

Attitude Control

Predicting the weather seems like a roll of the dice. Weather changes from day to day and from season to season. There are cold days in summer and hot days in winter. It's the weather. Now, how about moods? Have you ever noticed that sometimes your mood swings around randomly? Some minutes your emotions are rainy, and other times you are like a warm sunny day. The thing is, your moods affect others, especially your family. Maybe you can't control the weather, but you can control your mood. A bad attitude affects others around you and makes everyone walk on eggshells. People really let their moods fly around at home and end up hurting those they love most. But God has a different plan. He asks us to be self-controlled (1 Thessalonians 5:6) and He tells us that to truly love means we lay down our lives for others (John 15:13). He says to let the joy of the Lord be our strength (Nehemiah 8:10) and that every day that God makes (which is every day), we should rejoice and be glad (Psalm 118:24). He says to rejoice in the Lord always, then He says it again (in case you missed it)—Rejoice (Philippians 4:4)! Make an effort today to no longer let moods tell you how to feel. Let God tell you how to feel and change the atmosphere of your home to one of fun and love.

Where Did the Time Go?

I have a game on my phone that is addicting. That's right. I struggle in my addiction to a video game. I'm seeking help. Any chance I get, I am playing that game and when I'm not playing it, it's on my mind. I'm popping the little marbles even in my dreams and plotting to get to the next level. I'm Googling strategies. I have a problem. Here's the problem... the time I spend playing this game produces absolutely nothing for me or anyone. It's quite pointless, really. It's not relaxing and doesn't help me be a better father, husband, or preacher. Addictions distract us from being productive. God has given us His Word, Christ's blood, and even His own Spirit so we can change the world, not so we can get to the bonus round of a phone game. I'm not saying video games are evil, but be careful what is stealing your time. God has asked us to "redeem the time," to make every moment count (Ephesians 5:16). Hebrews 6:7 says, "Land that drinks in the rain often falling on it and that produces a crop useful to those for whom it is farmed receives the blessing of God." Let's limit our distractions together. Let's get out there and produce some fruit for God.

On Hold

Have you ever been praying for something and felt like you were on hold? Did you feel like you were listening to that on-hold music with the voice that says "Your call will be answered in the order in which it was received"? Have you ever wondered, *God, where are You?* In Exodus 3:7, God said to Moses, "I have heard (my people) crying out because of their slave drivers." When you pray, God hears you. In this story of Moses, we get a behind-the-scenes look at how God answers us. I wonder how long the Israelistes were crying out? They could've been thinking, "Is God hearing my prayer?" But the answer was already coming! God's plan took a bit of time. He had to get Moses on board and then get him in front of Pharaoh. Then, the plagues had to run their course. It took a while, but the answer was coming. The deliverance was already on its way. God may be working on your answer right now. When God sent Moses, many of the Israelites who were praying were like, "Well this guy can't possibly be the answer!" Remember that God's answer may not always follow your plan. But God has a better plan. He has heard you and He never asked you to quit praying. Jesus said "Ask and you shall receive" (Matthew 7:7). Keep praying and enjoy your on-hold music!

Goodness

In Exodus 33:19, as God prepares to show Himself to Moses, He says, "I will cause all my goodness to pass in front of you." Psalm 23:6 says, "Surely goodness and love will follow me all the days of my life." So, in these two verses, we see that God puts His goodness in front of us and His goodness is following us. That makes us like a goodness sandwich. Do you ever look ahead in your life at what's coming and say, *Uh Oh*, or look at the trail behind you and say *Whoops*? This is not God's plan for you. He wants to sow His goodness into your life in front of you. And then, He wants goodness to follow you as you allow His goodness to come out of you and into others. Now, what God calls *good* is really, really good. God's kind of good isn't just average, but it's limitless and indescribably, amazingly more than we can possibly fathom. That is the kind of goodness He wants flowing from you. So today, choose good and learn to leave a wake of goodness everywhere you go.

Shout FOR Joy

I bashed my toe into the corner of a wall the other day. I don't know if my feet are growing or if the wall moved, but it hurt. So, I shouted. A shout is the sound of an emotion expressing itself. Here, I was feeling pain. In Psalm 20:5, David writes, "We will shout for joy." This is an interesting way to word it. He did not say, "I will shout because of joy" or "I will shout because I'm happy." He said, "We will shout FOR joy" (emphasis mine). When I stubbed my toe, I shouted *because* of pain. I did not shout *for* pain. If I were shouting for pain, it would be weird. I did not want any more pain so I certainly wouldn't shout for it. But sometimes, we need more joy in our lives, like a smidge of happiness or an attitude adjustment. David says it helps to "shout for joy." If you need extra joy, say, "WHOOO HOOOO!" Don't you feel happier? Are we waiting for joy to come to us so that we can shout, or instead, do we do like David and when we need a little joy, we call for it with a shout? Your shout says, "Hey, I'm deciding to be happy!"

More than Enough

One day, about 5,000 men, plus women and children were hungry, but there were only five loaves of bread and two fish available to feed them all. How could this small meal feed so many? Matthew 14:19 says that Jesus took, "…the five loaves and the two fish and looking up to heaven, he gave thanks…." Then the disciples passed out the food and there was enough. Scripture goes on to say that after feeding everyone, there were 12 basketfuls of leftovers. What did Jesus do? He gave thanks and blessed the food. The blessing enabled the food to accomplish its purpose, which was a seemingly insurmountable task. I imagine if food could think, it would have been thinking, *I'm just too small.* Now, you are not food, but you do have a purpose. Like these five loaves, you may look at things in front of you and feel too small. But Ephesians 1 tells us that God has blessed you. That blessing means that the task in front of you is not too big. When you feel spent, like you have given all that you can and there is none of you left, remember that when Jesus blesses you, there isn't just enough—there is more than enough.

Excellence

What has God placed before you to do? What are you doing tomorrow? If you are going to school, then that is what God has placed before you in your life. Do you play a sport? Are you working tomorrow? What has God placed before you? Okay, now ask yourself, "Am I good at what I am doing?" Proverbs 22:29 says, "Do you see a skilled man in his work? He will serve before kings." The skilled man here found great success. Are you skilled at what you do? If you are going to school, become skillful at learning. Tell everyone around you to stop bugging you and embrace your textbooks. Read, even when it's not required. Study harder and become better at school then everyone else. Become better at your job than others. Become faster, smarter, more efficient. Become skilled. Get to work earlier and work longer. Notice the scripture doesn't ask if you like your work. I know there are things that you like to do and anyone can spend time becoming skillful at what they like to do. This proverb is asking you to become skillful at things you have to do. Create a pattern in your life of excellence in all things and you will find great promotion.

What Are You Doing Here?

In 1 Kings 19, the great prophet Elijah was running for his life. He was afraid he might be killed. He was visited by angels to be strengthened, and then God visited him and asked him in verse 9, "What are you doing here?" Elijah responded by saying that he was the only one in all of Israel left who still had not worshipped the false God, Baal. All the prophets had been killed and now he, himself, was on the run. You see, even a great prophet like Elijah was human and God revealed his humanity here to encourage us. Elijah was afraid and on the run. Has that ever happened to you? Did you ever feel like you were the only one all alone in your battles and no one was left on your side? Well, guess what? God is on your side. He will send His angels to strengthen you and then He will ask you, "What are you doing here?" He wants you back on track and He wants you to know you aren't alone. God told Elijah in verse 18, "Yet I reserve seven thousand in Israel—all whose knees have not bowed down to Baal." Elijah was not alone, and neither are you. God is strengthening you and God has a plan. Now, get back in there and do it!

Let's Get Excited

Some Sunday mornings, you wake up and you might be thinking, *Uggh… so sleepy. Oh yeah, I should go to church today.* Some go to church out of obligation while others skip it altogether. In the book of Ezra, we see the story of rebuilding the temple. In chapter 3, upon completing the foundation of the temple this is written, "And all the people gave a great shout of praise to the Lord" (v. 11). These people were excited to again have a place of worship and they were excited that they had helped build that place of worship. In fact, they were so excited, they shouted. It goes on to say in verse 13 that the sound was heard far away. It was like a huge party. When I tell my kids that we're going to Grandpa's house, they cheer. We should feel that way about going to our Father's house. Church, for some, has become a chore. They feel it's hard just getting there on time, if at all. But today, let's start a movement that changes that! The next time you're on your way to church, get cranked up! You're headed to your place of worship! Be thrilled about building your church. And when the neighbors say, "Hey, what's all that noise?" you can say, "Well, come see!"

The Wealth Tool

In Luke 16:9, Jesus said, "I tell you, use worldly wealth to gain friends for yourselves, so that when it is gone, you will be welcomed into eternal dwellings." Did Jesus just tell us to buy friends with money? Well then, what is Jesus saying? Jesus warned us about loving money and being greedy, so here He shows us a better way in which to view money. He said to "use worldly wealth," not shun it or be afraid of it. Money is just a tool. It cannot make you happy and it cannot save your soul. God placed gold in the Garden of Eden and it's on His streets in heaven. The gold is designed to be in the hands of those who will use it for God's purposes. God made Abraham very wealthy, knowing that wealth in the hands of a godly man is an effective tool. Proverbs 13:22 states, "…a sinner's wealth is stored up for the righteous." Money stored is pointless, but once it is given, it can feed children, build homes, dig wells, build churches, and help push the Gospel forward. Wealth is a tool. Don't be afraid to have it or to use it. Instead, be cautious that it doesn't ever have or use you.

Revived

Have you ever seen a defibrillator? Sounds like something you'd use to pump up tires, but it's not. A defibrillator is used to jump start a person whose heart has stopped. It is used to revive people. They put it on your chest and say, "Clear." *Boom!* You're revived. In Isaiah 57:15 God says, "I live in a high and holy place, but also with him who is contrite and lowly in spirit, to revive the spirit of the lowly and the heart of the contrite." God can revive you, no matter where you are. God explains in this verse that He lives at the top and the bottom. That's good because sometimes we might be on the bottom. When we are down, we often feel like God is so far away. But God says, "Hey, when you are down, I'm there too." He cares about you and He loves you. He loves you so much, that He goes on to say that He will revive you. You see, He's not just going to leave you down, but He is interested in lifting you back up. Let Him pick you up and give you His joy. He is all about reviving your heart. And when God revives you, well, you know it's a full charge. Ready? Clear...

Show Your Faith

In Mark 2, four men carried a guy who couldn't walk to Jesus, but the crowd was so big that they couldn't get inside. So they climbed up on the roof. It says in verse 4 that "...they made an opening in the roof above Jesus and, after digging through it, lowered the mat the paralyzed man was lying on." Well, the story goes on to tell how Jesus forgave this man his sins and healed him, but it makes a point to say in verse 5, "When Jesus saw their faith..." What did Jesus see? He saw a bunch of guys digging a hole in the roof while He was trying to teach. Now, I've never been in a church service where someone was so intent on getting in that they dug a hole through the roof. Here, Jesus shows us that faith often looks like hard work and perseverance (willingness to get your hands dirty). If you are praying to get into a good college, then work hard in school and study. Need a job? Get out there and apply yourself. Praying for your marriage? Excellent! Go buy your wife some flowers. Show Jesus your faith by what you do. Start digging that hole.

Coming to You

Ezekiel 12:1 starts by saying, "The word of the LORD came to me." I love that phrase. It is so confident. How cool that God was talking to Ezekiel and he knew it. I mean, when God talks to you and you are sure it's Him, well then you can have amazing faith in what He has said. When we receive Christ, we have access to this kind of confidence. Before Christ, a prophet was said to have the Spirit of the Lord upon him so that the people would receive the word of the Lord. But Christ has made this same Spirit available to anyone who will believe. In Acts 2, the Holy Spirit came and filled the 120 believers in the upper room and then Peter quoted the prophet Joel to explain what was happening as he said that the Lord would pour out His Spirit on all people, and they would prophesy (Acts 2:17). Just think how that changes the world. Instead of just one guy tearing it up, now God has a bunch of us out there speaking the words He shares with us; a whole army. What are you working on in your life now? Do you need help? Do you need wisdom? Well, ask God, and then listen for His voice. The word of the Lord can come to you, and then, don't forget to do what He says!

Independence

Ah, Independence Day. At a time like this, it is important to remember why we are America and by who's might we were founded. America was first colonized as a religious refuge where people could worship God freely. Later, as America declared its freedom, they were also declaring war against England, which was, at that time, the most powerful of all nations. It would have appeared to the entire world that the colonists had signed their own death sentence by committing high treason. America's army was new, untrained and outnumbered. Yet, they prevailed. Why? Was it because Americans were so passionate and fought so hard? Passion alone would not be enough to prevail against such incredible odds. There are a great many revolutionary battles that document the invisible hand of God acting in accord with our forefather's bravery and zeal. Only by the miraculous power of God do we exist as a free nation today. In 1787, Benjamin Franklin is quoted saying, *"In the beginning of the contest with G. Britain, when we were sensible of danger, we had daily prayer in this room for the Divine protection—our prayers, Sir, were heard, and they were graciously answered. ... I have lived, Sir, a long time; and the longer I live, the more convincing proofs I see of this truth, that God governs the affairs of men!"* It is America's commitment to allow its citizens to worship God freely that has paved the way for hundreds of other nations to hold the same principles about religious freedom. Let's not only celebrate the Americans who fought for our freedom but let's celebrate God who gave us the freedom and the victory.

Reading the Good Stuff

Have you seen the size of kids' fiction books lately? There are stories of Pegasus and swords, of myths and legends that have the young people tackling books that approach the thickness of a Bible. And, they are being read. Ok—so how about that Bible? We know you can read thick books, and fast. Some of you get through a book in a few days. The Bible isn't as hard to read as you might think. Listen to this. In Habakkuk 2:2 God says, "Write down the revelation and make it plain on tablets so that a herald may run with it." You have a race to run, a destiny to fulfill, and although reading about myths and flying cattle may be fun, it isn't the key to winning in life. Now, I'm not saying not to read these types of books. I'm encouraging you to also read the Bible. This is the book you need to read and run with. It shows you where the hurdles are and gets you up the mountain (or even moving the mountains). Habakkuk 2:14 goes on to say, "For the earth will be filled with the knowledge of the glory of the Lord." That knowledge needs to find its way into your heart. Grab your Bible, press into it, and run with it.

Dwell

Have you ever been home, but you weren't really home? You were distracted with thinking about other things and were off somewhere else in your mind. It's hard for you to connect to others, when even though you are there, you aren't really there. Psalm 84:4 says, "Blessed are those who dwell in your house; they are ever praising you." God's house is church, and blessed are those who dwell there. Those who dwell are described as those who are ever praising God. When we go to church, are we really there? Or, are we distracted? Sometimes we find ourselves thinking, "When is the music going to finish so we can get to the sermon?" But God is saying that dwelling in His house means your thoughts are on Him. You're not distracted, but you're in the moment with our Lord and Savior. This scripture is actually a line from a song. It is to be sung. Are we skipping the singing part of church? When we get to church, let's all get excited about dwelling with God and getting our thoughts fixed on Jesus and really singing to God. Let's be that group of people God describes as "ever praising." When you are at church, *be* at church. It is the house of God and blessed is he who dwells there.

Best Place Ever

Have you ever heard the scripture, "Better is one day in your courts than a thousand elsewhere" (Psalm 84:10)? Did you ever think about why is it better? Because God has designed us to be with Him. He designed us to be in His presence and in His house. Want to know what the next line in the scripture is after that one? Here you go… it says "I would rather be a doorkeeper in the house of my God than dwell in the tents of the wicked" (v. 11). God is instructing us to serve in His house, to find some way to be helpful. Someone has to open the door, and the doorkeeper is the first person who greets when someone comes in seeking God. Lately, more people are looking for places to give back and to serve. The local church, God's house, has many places for you to volunteer. At church, there are children who need to hear the stories of Christ and there are babies to watch so that young parents can grow in the Lord. The next time you are at church, look around at all the areas that could use you.

Slipping

Your day today serves a purpose. You are going somewhere, moving, and it does not count for nothing. Your day counts, and what you do matters. Sometimes we get discouraged, worried, and anxiety tries to freeze us. But God wants you to stay at it, be diligent, faithful, and keep on trying. He desires for you to win. Psalm 94:18-19 says, "When I said, 'My foot is slipping,' your love, O LORD, supported me. When anxiety was great within me, your consolation brought joy to my soul." God can supply whatever we need when we need it. We shouldn't be afraid to tell God, "Hey, I'm slipping here." When temptation comes, and you start down the wrong road, turn to the Lord and say, "Slipping." Or in troubled waters, when the ground gives way under you and it looks like you're going to lose say, "Hey God, I'm slipping." I think sometimes we forget to cry out for God's help. Remember, His consultation brings joy to our soul. He's with you right now. He isn't leaving you in your mess, but He wants to be exactly what you need so that you can keep on keeping on. Let go of anxiety and believe God. His love is supporting you always.

Who's Going to Church?

Acts 14:1 says, "At Iconium Paul and Barnabas went as usual into the synagogue. There they spoke so effectively that a great number of Jews and Gentiles believed." So what were Paul and Barnabas speaking about? Well, they were preaching and teaching about Jesus. This verse says that Paul and Barnabas usually went to the synagogue. In fact, as you follow them through the book of Acts, that is exactly where they went in each city. The synagogue today is called church. If you want to hear some good preaching, teaching, gain some faith, learn about grace, and find salvation, where would you go today? That's right, you'd go to church. God hasn't changed. He is still interested in getting people into His church. When Mary and Joseph went searching for Jesus, they finally found him at church. Jesus said to them in Luke 2:49, "Why were you searching for me?...Didn't you know that I had to be in my Father's house." If you have gotten out of the habit of going to church, well, reconsider. It's where Paul and Barnabas would go, and it's where Jesus will be.

Goodness, Then Knowledge

Second Peter 1:5 says to add to your goodness, knowledge. Ok, so there is an order to things. If this were like a recipe or something, this tells you that you should start with some goodness. Do you have some goodness? If this recipe called for eggs and you didn't have any, you'd have to go get some. Goodness is the desire to do the right thing. Do you have that? Great. Now we want to add to that knowledge. This gives you the idea that you have some learning to do. Don't be afraid to dig in and learn. Some of the greatest minds ever discovered God as they studied creation and science. You see knowledge—real truth—never disagrees with God or His Word. Some teachers might say that God is a myth, but you should know on many levels why they are wrong. Arm yourself against this deception. Christians should be learned and knowledgeable. We need to be able to be able to have a conversation with the lost and to discuss the Bible, having a firm footing in what we believe. The best knowledge you can get comes from the Word of God. It is the only solid truth to build your life upon.

In Your Shoes

Sometimes people might tell you they know how you feel. You might be thinking, "No one could possibly know how I feel unless they spent a day in shoes." Then, when no one knows what you are feeling, you feel isolated, alone. Sure, you're a Christian, but does that mean you are invincible and unshakeable? When we are knocked down, we are reminded of our humanity. I mean, we are flesh and blood, and when we get cut, we bleed. Hebrews 2:14 says, "Since the children have flesh and blood, he too shared in their humanity...." "He" is referring to Jesus. Christ took on the form of a man. He became a part of humanity, not just dropping by to lead the charge, but He became one of us. He became human. He put your shoes on. Jesus knows how you feel and He experienced even greater suffering in order that those who would believe in Him wouldn't have to. He became poor so that you might be rich. He took sickness and disease upon Himself so that by His stripes, you are healed. He defeated death so that you wouldn't be afraid. You are never alone. He knows exactly how you feel and has overcome all on your behalf.

All the World—Seriously?

The Great Commission is quite a commission. Jesus said in Matthew 28:19-20, "Go and make disciples of all nations, baptizing them in the name of the Father and of the Son and of the Holy Spirit, and teaching them to obey everything I have commanded you." Well, that is quite overwhelming. Christ is calling us to tell others about Him and His message. Really, where would you be without Jesus and what He has done in your life? Christ wants us to share that. I think sometimes we think of reaching the whole world as quite overwhelming, but truth is you don't have to get on a plane and go to Africa to tell someone about Jesus. There are people who don't know Jesus next door to your house, in the cubicle down the hall, or at your family reunion. Pray and ask God for the right opportunity to tell them about Him. Invite others to church or tell them about a great Christian radio station you listen to. Remember also that when you give a financial gift to help your church or other Christian organization, your gift to God is working as a seed to reach the lost and to preach the message of Christ to the world. If we all do a little, then God does a lot.

Talking Nonsense

When I was a kid, I learned a great little rhyme that goes, "Ring around the rosie, pockets full of posies, ashes, ashes, we all fall down." I had no idea what that was supposed to mean, but the ashes part always made me think that something burnt and then I would fall down. Or maybe you're more familiar with the story of the cute little egg man (Humpty Dumpty) who fell off the wall. And don't forget that the London Bridge is falling down. Seems like we'd say anything if it is in nursery rhyme form… Psalm 91:2 says, "I will say of the LORD 'He is my refuge and my fortress, my God in whom I trust.'" Try saying that out loud, instead of a bunch of nonsense. You see, it matters what we are saying and this is the kind of stuff God wants us saying. Ponder the kinds of things we speak through the day, things like, "I'm broke. I got no money left. I don't know what I'm going to do now. This is never going to work. Oh just my luck! Where is God?" What if instead of saying that kind of stuff, which just brings us and others down, what if we looked at our problem and then said, "God is my refuge, and I trust in Him"? Well that feels a lot better, doesn't it?

Lavish

When you think of the word "lavish," what do you think of? Lavish is like more than you or anyone would ever need. For instance, if you put salt on something, it's different than if you lavished salt on it. Oops, way too salty. Or, if you lavished frosting on a cake, the cake-to-frosting ratio might be off a bit, but boy, would it taste good. How about a house that is lavish? You get an image of all the finest furniture and décor. First John 3:1 says, "How great is the love the Father has lavished on us." Ephesians 1:7 says, "In him we have redemption through his blood, the forgiveness of sins, in accordance with the riches of God's grace that he lavished on us." God has given us His love and His grace, and He didn't skimp. It isn't just enough love. It's extravagant, overwhelming love. It's the finest love and it's more love than you can comprehend. And His grace? You may think you are a mess sometimes, especially when you think about where you came from. But God's grace is lavished on you. His grace brings the finest and purest forgiveness and He has more grace than you need. This is how God gives when He gives to us. He isn't just giving you enough, He's lavishing.

Speak Lord, Your Servant Is Listening

Samuel grew up in the tabernacle of God. One day, he heard a voice that woke him up. The voice said, "Samuel, Samuel..." Samuel thought it was Eli, the priest, calling for him. Eli was like a dad to Samuel; he was raising him. But the voice wasn't Eli. This happened three times, when finally Eli realized it must be God calling the boy. So Eli told Samuel that the next time he heard the voice, he should say, "Speak, Lord, for Your servant is listening." As you grow up, there are many voices telling you what to do, what is right, and what is wrong, and telling you what to believe. But at some point, you must learn to hear from God for yourself. As we grow, we cannot always rely on the Eli's in our lives. It's good for us to have godly friends and mentors, but Samuel's story reminds us that at some point, we need to get to know God for ourselves. Maybe the Eli's in your life make you go to church, but there comes a time when you should want to go to church. I tell you to read the Bible, but there comes a moment when *you* should desire to read the Bible. Open up your Bible and pray, "Speak Lord, for Your servant is listening." Then be prepared to hear from God.

Lover of Money?

You know how many songs are written about money? The world sure makes a big deal about money. But money isn't important, right? Well, without money in the church, there would be no buildings or no ministries to reach others for Christ. And how are we supposed to help the hurting if we can't even pay our own bills? Don't think I'm receiving an offering right now, I just want to warn you of the other side of money. Ecclesiastes 5:10 warns, "Whoever loves money never has money enough." Satan has a trap for us. The trap is to get us wanting more and more, thinking we never have enough money for our own wants and desires. Now you work for money and you spend money, but how can you find out if you're a lover of money? The best defense against loving money is to become a giver. Sow some seed. When you put your own needs behind the needs of others and begin to give to the Lord, you are in essence sending a message that God is your priority. As you sow seed, God will be faithful to bring you a harvest, and then you'll find yourself in a position to give even more. Sure, you have needs, but put God's needs first, and then all these things will be added to you.

Straight Paths

I was driving to California to go to the beach, and man, the roads were winding around and turning. Freeway exits had me looping in circles. I was checking my phone for a map (which isn't super safe to do while driving) and I was wishing there was just a straight road right to the beach. Life can be like this trip, taking you this way then that, with plenty of U-turns in between. Sometimes I think we just accept our life's twists and turns and mountains thinking that's the way it is supposed to be. But according to the Bible, life doesn't have to be like that. Jesus taught us to move mountains with our faith. Psalm 27:11 says "Teach me your way O LORD, lead me in a straight path." Ah, a straight path. This doesn't mean that God is magically changing the actual freeway for me, although that would be quite cool; the path He is talking about is my life, my purpose, my destiny. It is the road I'm on as I grow and change and head into the Promised Land. The key is to allow God to teach us His ways. His way is straight, and His way wins. The next time the twists and turns of your road confuse you just remember, God's path for you isn't confusing; you may just have some more learning to do.

Resistance

I think some of the greatest resistance we have as we move with God comes from other people. It was the king who threw Daniel in the lion's den. It was the Philistines who were forever attacking Israel. It was Jesus' own people who wanted Him crucified. People are not always going to be excited about your success. When Joseph was given a nice new robe, his brothers hated him for it. While we are told to love people anyway, Jesus also warned us in Matthew 7:6, "Do not give dogs what is sacred; do not throw your pearls to pigs." Jesus was telling us not to entrust our most important and valuable things to just anyone. Our hopes, dreams, and our inner parts are reserved for the Lord. People won't always be rooting for you, but don't let that get you down. Jesus told us we would suffer some persecution because of Him. Keep your eyes fixed on Christ. Pray for those who persecute you. Love everyone and keep running your race. Don't be discouraged by people, but be encouraged by the Lord. So when the boss is on you or your friends bag on you, just remember that if God is for you, it doesn't matter who might be against you. Do that, and you won't be quitting, you'll just keep running.

Is Reading the Bible Really Important?

The Bible has a lot of information in it. Every passage seems to have wisdom and information as deep as the ocean. When you first receive Christ, you know that the Bible is important to study, but then life gets busy. One danger of not studying the Word, however, is that someone may tell you something that isn't true and you may believe it. This could leave you headed the wrong way. Romans 10:17 tells us that faith comes by hearing God's Word. Hebrews 4:14 says, "Let us hold firmly to the faith we profess." These verses give us an important pattern to follow. As we study the Bible, it gives us more of the faith that we can then hold onto firmly. You should know from God's Word exactly what you believe. Then when a wrong message comes your way, the Spirit within you can say, "No, that isn't what the Bible says." There are an awful lot of worldviews and religious opinions about God. Many of them differ from one another, but the truth is written in the Word. The Word of God is like an anchor for our lives. It is the rock we build upon so that we aren't shaken. What an awesome opportunity we have every day to read the Word of God.

Hold on to Your Faith

We saw yesterday that Hebrews 4:14 says, "Let us hold firmly to the faith we profess." Okay, so you have a faith that you profess—Jesus is Lord. But what else do you believe about Jesus? Well, in your faith you might say that Jesus saves. What, exactly, does He save you from? Well, He rescues you from sin and death. Okay, what else? You see, as you find out more about what God does and desires in our lives from reading the Word, it then becomes important that we apply what we've learned. By applying it to our lives, we hold on to it. So when something happens in life that is different from what God has promised or is different than what Jesus brought you, you need to hold on to your faith. Hold firmly. In fact, profess that faith. Don't believe the lies that Satan and this world bring you, but say, "No, that is not God's plan. Jesus died so that I wouldn't have to experience this in my life." Hold on to your faith. Don't be shaken by the world's circumstances and storms, but be anchored in the fact that God is bigger. Be confident that Jesus has completed the work and that anything contrary to God's Word has been crucified and is powerless.

God Our Salvation

Have you ever stared defeat in the face and thought, *Well this is it, I lose.* Did it seem like everything was impossible? I imagine that is exactly how Moses could have felt as he found himself and the nation of Israel hemmed in by the mountains, the Red Sea, and pursued by the Egyptian army. He could have said, "Well, it was a good run, but it's over now." But Moses trusted God, and God performed the impossible. Afterward, Moses sang this song in Exodus 15:2, "The LORD is my strength and my song; he has become my salvation." A running theme in the Word of God is that God is interested in bringing us salvation. Salvation applies to every area of potential death and destruction in your life. Moses' salvation included release from oppression and deliverance of an entire nation from slavery. Jesus also came to set captives free and the captivity we are in today affects many areas of our lives. God desires to become our salvation. Jesus saved us from death itself so that anyone who believes in Him has everlasting life. Now, problems will still come, but remember God's role in all of this. He is not the problem but instead, He is the salvation.

Not by Chance

Have you ever randomly turned on the radio or TV and happened upon a station where some guy was talking about God? Or have you ever picked up a book and started reading, only to realize it was about God? Here's the thing—I don't believe you did that by chance. I believe it all happened as part of a plan that began before you were born. You need answers. You've heard this or that about God or Jesus, but right now something very real is happening. Jesus is knocking on the door of your heart. It feels like a tugging inside of you. God who created you is wanting you to let Him into your life. And doing so is a simple decision. You don't have to suddenly be perfect to know Him. You just have to believe in Jesus and believe that God loves you. He sent His Son, Jesus, to bring you forgiveness. Jesus died on the cross so you could have that forgiveness, and then He rose from the dead, bringing you a new life and a brand new start. Do you need a new start? Well, have you ever prayed before? Here is the greatest prayer you could ever pray: "Father forgive me of my sins. Jesus come into my heart and be my Lord and Savior. Jesus is Lord." Believe it and be ready for your brand new start.

Pray Expectantly

Do you ever pray for happiness in the midst of a problem? Let's think about it—what is a problem, anyway? A problem is an opportunity to win. With that perspective, it makes it easier to understand why God commands us to rejoice in the Lord always. So the answer to your prayer for happiness comes when you choose to obey and rejoice regardless of the problem. In Psalm 5:3 David prays, "In the morning, O Lord, you hear my voice; in the morning I lay my requests before you and wait in expectation." Notice that David is praying to God with some requests, but how does he wait? Does he wait in angst and worry? Is he waiting in despair or continuing his cries? No! There is a secret to answered prayer right here. He is waiting in expectation. He is expecting an answer. Now when a woman is pregnant, she is expecting. Maybe she cannot hold the baby in her arms yet, but she knows the baby is coming. Her expectation has her preparing a place for the baby to sleep and buying some little diapers, too. When you pray, expect the answer is already yours. You just can't see it yet. When you pray this way, it is easy to rejoice in the midst of a problem because you know that God has already provided the answer. It's there. The answer is already there.

Change Me

Prayer changes things. No question that as a Christian, your prayer life is an important part of every day. But how should we pray? Jesus taught the disciples what we call the Lord's Prayer. Let's think about some of the phrases of that prayer.

> "Give us this day our daily bread." (Daily bread is the wisdom of God revealed in His Word.)
> "Forgive us our debt as we forgive others."
> "Deliver us from evil."

You'll notice from these phrases, this prayer is not about asking God for stuff or to change other people. It's about asking God to help us change, and to grow individually. It's asking the Lord to help us learn His wisdom and ways. It's asking God to forgive us as we forgive others and help us to not fall into the traps of sin. So often, we are praying asking God to change the circumstances of our lives, but Jesus is teaching us that if we allow God to change us, our circumstances in life will change. We mostly think of prayer as a plea for God to fix our problems, which it can be. But Jesus had another option. Allow God to fix you.

Good News

I'll bet there wasn't much good news on the newscast today. There was probably a bit of doom and gloom. But I have some good news. Things are getting better. Think about this good news. James 2:5 says, "Has not God chosen those who are poor in the eyes of the world to be rich in faith and to inherit the kingdom he promised those who love him." You see, God's character is to take you from wherever you are to somewhere better. Think about it. He brought the Israelites out of slavery and into a Promised Land. He chose David the shepherd boy to be king. Along the way there may still be challenges, but God's ultimate plan is for you is to take you somewhere better. Jesus brought good news to the poor. The government may not always have good news for the poor, but God does. What is this good news for the poor? God is bringing you into His kingdom, where there is abundance and more than you can contain. It is a land flowing with milk and honey. Your job is to believe it is possible. Wherever you are, God has good news for you. He is making you rich in faith and you are an heir of the Kingdom of God. You are sons and daughters of the King.

Pure Joy

Everyone has bad days, but what makes the day bad? Could the goodness or badness of a day be determined by our response to circumstances? James 1:2-3 says, "Consider it pure joy, my brothers, whenever you face trials of many kinds,because you know that the testing of your faith develops perseverance." There are some situations that will cause us to mourn, like when Jesus went to where the body of his friend Lazarus lay in a grave, Jesus wept. God gave us tears and emotions because it is okay to cry. But after we've mourned, then what? If we stay in our mourning too long, it can become depression. This isn't what God wants for us. Jesus told us that in life, there will be storms. He was saying that there are going to be problems and battles. Our job isn't to assign blame or get knocked down. Our job is to consider it all joy. Actually, not just joy, but pure joy. Pure joy is like bliss, utter contentment. Why would we consider it fun when junk happens? Well, because we are learning to be stronger. So when the devil goes out of his way trying to change your attitude, make sure he knows that you are going to be just fine. In a trial, we have that ability to experience gain, development, and wisdom. Children are often scared in thunderstorms, but adults aren't often scared. Why? It's because adults have learned through experience that after all the rain and noise, the sun will come out again. If we can refuse fear in the midst of trial, and instead look at the mess and say to ourselves, "Bring it on, I'm still happy"—if we can truly learn to consider our trial a joy, a pure joy, then every trial we face will no longer have any power over us.

In the Army

Ephesians 6:11 instructs us to, "Put on the full armor of God so that you can take your stand against the devil's schemes." Whoa there! Hey, that sounds like work! Battle? Armor? I don't think I signed up for this. No, I signed up for easy going Christianity. Yeah, well guess what? When you receive Christ, you enlist in the army of the Lord. This is a much better life, full of victory, territory, wells you did not dig, and cities you did not build, but God never promised you it would be a picnic. So, let's talk about this armor. There is a helmet of salvation that protects your thoughts. There is a shield of faith to ward off the enemy's bullets. There is the sword of the spirit, which is God's Word. The Word of God you speak becomes a weapon, just like when Jesus quoted the word at Satan during His temptation (Matthew 4). There is a belt of truth which is the seed of truth that God produces in our hearts. We have our feet fitted with the readiness that comes from the gospel of peace. The gospel of peace is the truth that Jesus has made a way and won the war. This means my feet are ready to win. There is a breastplate of righteousness, because the enemy will try to attack your heart saying you aren't good enough. The truth is that the righteousness of Jesus makes you good enough—that truth protects your heart like a breastplate. God has given you a whole uniform of protection. You've been recruited to God's army to tell others about the Lord. Now march!

Forget About It

In Hebrews 10:17, God says, "Their sins and lawless acts I will remember no more." That promise is for you and me. Many times we are waiting to get our lives just right so that we can talk to God or start going to a church. The enemy is going to plant thoughts in our minds that we are no good, accusing us of being a hypocrites, or he may say that everyone else is a hypocrite so we want no part of it. Whether we focus on our own sin or the sins of others, we keep ourselves distracted from the truth and separated from God. The truth is that God has forgotten your sin. You have to forget too. A lot of times we find ourselves pointing out other people's sins because we have not yet forgiven ourselves. But God has forgiven you and those around you. You might say, *But Jason, you have no idea what I've done.* You're right, and you don't know what I've done. We may remember, but God doesn't remember, and so neither should we. God wants us free of our guilt so we are able to serve Him and even draw more near to Him. When we are feeling guilty, we push God away because we are ashamed. In the same way, when we stand in judgment of others, we build a wall between ourselves and God. The blood of Jesus washed away all sin. Let's all make a decision to accept what Jesus has done and no longer dwell in the past of what if, or I wish. Instead, let's look at our bright new future with God and start a new day, free of guilt, condemnation, and shame.

It's Not My Fault

When my car broke down, I took it to the shop to find out what was wrong. The mechanic told me that a belt had broken. Now, I didn't break the belt. So who should have to pay to get my car fixed? That broken belt wasn't my fault. I shouldn't have to pay for the repair. Thankfully, that didn't really happen, but sometimes we live our lives with that attitude. When something breaks in our life, we have the opportunity to fix it and move to another level. But there is a great phrase we use to stunt our own growth, and it sounds like this: "It's not my fault." Maybe what happened wasn't your fault, but when you fall in a pit, a crisis, or a storm, you have the opportunity to look at the situation and determine what you can do to make sure this never happens again. Is there something in your actions, your way of thinking, or your faith in God that needs adjusting? If you constantly view yourself as a victim of your problems, then you will never change. A victim, by definition, is slave to the crisis. A victim is actually forced to serve the problem. Refusing to be a victim means you seize the authority to make changes and solve problems. Many people in the Bible found a way to succeed, despite ungodly circumstances (think of Joseph and Daniel). In every crisis, find a way to be personally accountable for your attitude. With God's help, you can fix what is broken.

Need a Miracle?

Do you need a miracle? If so, you are in luck. God is in the business of doing miracles. But don't take my word for it, just check the Bible. God performed all kinds of miracles like walking on water and parting the Red Sea. Do you need a financial miracle? God multiplies stuff. He multiplied food and made it so that oil and flour didn't run out. He brought money out of a fish mouth and had a whole boatload of fish jump in a net. Need healing? God sent His word, and it has healed you. Jesus healed sick, blind, and even dead people. God's Word holds the entire universe together. Just think about all that was created when God threw out these simple words: "Let there be!" Are you in a battle? No problem. God has sent legions of angels in chariots of fire to fight for His children. Entire wars have been won without God's children even having to fight. The enemy destroyed themselves! One time, God even stopped the rotation of the earth so that it would stay light longer while His children prevailed in victory. God does miracles. He's supernatural like that. He is unstoppable, immoveable, unshakable, omnipotent, alpha and omega, beginning and end. And not only does He do miracles, but He is your Father and He wants to care for you. Not because you have done everything right, but because you have chosen to believe in Jesus, you qualify for a miracle today. Do you believe it? Then receive your miracle. Stand firm knowing that the answer has already come!

Love Your Enemies

Jesus told us in Matthew 5:44 to love our enemies and pray for those who persecute us. Jesus called us to do more and love more than what is normal. If someone is mean to you, then you naturally want to be mean back. But what if you were nice to nearly everyone and friendly with all, complimenting and encouraging and praying for everyone you came into contact with? A business knows that it must provide consistently friendly service in order to be successful. Why? Because one angry person will tell seven people who in turn tell three more each, making 22 people who are mad at your business. When you are unfriendly or talking bad about someone and make them mad, you are potentially creating 22 people who think that you are mean. As Christians, how can we influence people if they don't like us? Instead, we need to be friendly with everyone. If kids are making fun of a different kid, don't get involved. Be quiet. If you are friendly, happy, and present yourself confidently, then people will begin to know you and like you. It is true that nearly everyone around you is feeling insecure and awkward. What if you walked in a room and encouraged others? In doing this, the goal isn't to be popular; the goal is to obey Christ. By your obedience, you gain influence, and with influence you can begin to lead others, which is something we Christians should be doing. Love everyone, even your enemies.

Moved by Compassion

In Mark 1, a man with leprosy came to Jesus and begged Him on his knees saying, "If you are willing, you can make me clean. Filled with compassion, Jesus reached out His hand and touched the man. 'I am willing,' he said. 'Be clean!'" (1:40-41). Immediately, the man was healed. Wow. What moved Christ to perform this amazing miracle? Scripture tells us that He was moved by compassion. As Christians, we are to be imitators of God, followers of Christ. But sometimes we get so busy that we miss the opportunity to see someone else's need; we lack compassion. Throughout the Gospels, Jesus was moved by compassion, and that compassion often led to a great work of God— like raising the dead, healings, and even feeding 5,000-plus people. For Jesus, compassion was the norm. It was a characteristic that defined Him. He saw what people needed and found a way to meet that need. Look for the needs around you and let compassion stir in your heart and move you. Then, watch the power of God partner with you to meet those needs so that He gets the glory. Jesus was moved by compassion and we should be, too.

Givers

Chores…gotta love them. "Now when you wash the car, make sure you *blah, blah, blah*." Notice, it's not a question of *whether* you are going to wash the car, the instruction concerns what you will do *while* washing it. Jesus said in Matthew 6:2, "So when you give to the needy, do not announce it with trumpets…." Jesus wasn't asking us to give to the needy. That much was expected. He was telling us how to give when He said, "When you give…" In John 13, when Judas left to go betray Jesus, the disciples thought he had left the group to give some money to the poor. They thought that since he was in charge of the purse for Jesus, that Jesus had told him to go give some money away. For the disciples to think that, it must have happened before. In fact, for them to naturally jump to the assumption that Judas was just going off to give some money away for Jesus, it must have happened often. Jesus was a giver and He expects us be givers, too. Giving is an important part of our Christianity—tithes, offerings, and alms for the poor, the widow, and the orphan. Giving helps keep us balanced and it helps us keep a proper perspective on money. Jesus was a giver and we must be givers, too.

Sacrifice

In John 10:18, Jesus said, "No one takes [my life] from me, but I lay it down of my own accord. I have authority to lay it down and authority to take it up again." It's important to know that Jesus was crucified on His terms, according to the Father's will. He could have stopped the process at any time and called in legions of angels, but instead He willingly allowed the people to crucify Him. His life was not taken from Him; He gave it up for us. This is the ultimate sacrifice. We can learn from this. You don't need to die for the sins of the world; Jesus already did that. But a willingness to give up we want in order to help others, this is our sacrifice. There's lots of stuff you want to do or buy, or there are lots of places you want to go. When you come home from a hard day, you want to do nothing but rest—but a good man lays down his needs. A dad just wants to go to the couch and have the remote, maybe some chips, but instead he invests time in his family. A mom wakes up at 2 a.m. to feed her baby because she puts the baby's needs above her need for sleep. A friend forgets his own needs to help his friend. This is a better way to live. Jesus paved the way by His example, and this way leads to life. Jesus was willing to sacrifice; we should be too.

Be Bold

A strong characteristic we see in Christ was boldness. Jesus wasn't some wimpy, pushed around, beaten down dude. For example, in Luke 13, Jesus was teaching in the synagogue, when He saw a woman who was crippled, so He healed her. Well, it happened to be the Sabbath, so a synagogue leader got all uptight and told people that no healing should happen on the Sabbath. His suggestion was that the woman come get healed some other day. So what did Jesus do in response to this rebuke? Did He cower? Apologize? Nope. He replied by saying, "You hypocrites! You would untie and feed a donkey on the Sabbath, but you don't think it's okay to set a woman free whom Satan has bound for 18 years?" (my paraphrase of v. 15-16). Jesus showed courage here—courage to defend the weak, courage to stand for what is right, the kind of courage and fervor that clears out a temple with a whip, if need be. When it comes to the truth of God, we can be bold. If someone is striking you on the cheek, then sure, turn the other cheek. But if they are attacking the weak or perpetrating injustice, then like Jesus, take off the gloves and get bold. Jesus was bold for our sake, so we can be bold for Him.

The Wisdom that Leads to Life

Jesus knew the answers. Whatever questions were asked, He knew the answers. In Matthew 22:15-22, Jesus was asked a question about paying taxes to Caesar. When He gave His response, it says that those who heard Him were amazed and marveled at His teaching. What they were marveling at was His wisdom. When Jesus was on earth, we know that people were amazed at the miracles they saw like lame men walking and the blind seeing, but they were also amazed by Jesus' wisdom. This same wisdom is in the teachings we study. In the Bible, we are given the very wisdom of God. He has given us His Word so that we might know all of the truth and have the right answers for this world's questions. Many people at your school, work, or in your neighborhood need life and you have the answers that lead to life. You have access to God's wisdom. If you want to find out what Jesus would do, you should study His teachings so that you can share that wisdom. Jesus was wise, and you and I can be wise too.

Inside and Out

How do you look today? Man judges by the outward appearance; it says so in 1 Samuel 16:7. People can't see your heart, so they decide what you are like by looking at you. That sounds superficial, and it certainly doesn't sound Christian. Sometimes we say things like, "Well, I don't care what others think about me." Now it's true, we shouldn't be trying to please people, we should please God. But I think there's a better balance we can strike. Luke 2:52 says that Jesus grew in favor with both God and men. From this verse, I get the idea Jesus took care of how He looked, inside and outside. We are all uniquely beautiful, regardless of what the world calls beautiful. God has given us this physical body. We should take care of it the way we steward over anything God gives us by getting a bit of exercise, eating better, and taking a shower every now and again. But the inner beauty of who you are—your character, honor, loyalty, and integrity—are far more important than how you look. Let's follow the example of Jesus, who took care of Himself inside and out, and so should we.

Help Them All

We see in Matthew 12:15 that many followed Jesus, and Hehealedall-their sick. First, notice that many followed. Not everyone followed, but many did. Some people are going to reject Jesus, even if they see Him in person. The verse goes on to say that Jesus healed all their sick. He healed all of them. Jesus said that He only did what He saw the Father do and He only did the will of God. From this truth, we can gather that it was God's will to heal **all** of their sick, and so Jesus did it. He didn't just heal a few. He never said, "Well, I'm not going to heal you. And I don't know about you, either. I'm not sure what you'll do with this healing...maybe it's not God's will for you to be healed." I think this is an important bit of wisdom. When we come across people we can serve, help, or love, we should be willing to help all, like Jesus. We should be willing to pray for any, to give a helping hand, and to speak the seed of God while we do it. Jesus was teaching truth, and then helping others. Jesus was willing to help everyone. Age, social status, or color didn't matter. We can do this too.

Joy

Have you ever been happy, but then someone came along and ruined it all? In John 15:11, Jesus said, "I have told you this so that my joy may be in you and that your joy may be complete." Jesus wants you to have His joy. His joy is different than regular joy. Regular joy happens because things are going well, but then if things aren't going well, no more joy. Jesus has a different kind of joy. Jesus' joy can remain through it all. You might say, "Well that's impossible, how can I be happy when I'm hurting?" The cool thing about God's ways is that God is in the business of doing what seems impossible. Hebrews 12:2 says, "Let us fix our eyes on Jesus, the author and perfecter of our faith, who for thejoysetbeforeHim endured the cross." You see, the joy that Jesus gives stays deep in your heart, no matter what is going on. Even the suffering Jesus endured on the cross could not erase His joy. This kind of joy only comes from Christ. It comes as we learn to obey His most important command, which is to love others as He loved us and laid His life down for us. Jesus displayed joy and He's given that joy to you!

Build Others Up to Win

Do you like to win? Well, obviously no one likes to lose. We are, by nature, competitive. We want to know we are better at stuff than others. In fact, sometimes we want to know we are the best—the most important employee in the company or the key player on the team so that the company will fall apart if we leave or the team won't survive a game if we don't show. But, this is more of a world attitude. Jesus showed us a different way. From the time He started His ministry, He began to develop those around him, teaching them to do what He did. He showed the disciples how to preach, how to pray, how to live and then He sent them out to minister on their own. He watched them. He gave them all the tools He had to give. He desired for them to win. He even encouraged them to do greater things than He had done. We can do this. We can develop those around us and desire for them to win. Help another sales associate land the big deal or help your sister do the dishes, or help a teammate score a goal. It won't make you worse to make others better. Help raise others up, encourage them to try. Want them to win! This is how Jesus did it, and we can too.

Be Honest

Do you ever find yourself saying, "I promise, no I really promise. I swear. As God is my witness...." Or have you ever said, "Ooh, I can't make it today, I'm...uhh, not feeling good, I swear." When we want someone to believe us, we promise and swear. But Jesus had a different approach. In Matthew 5, He told us not to make a big hoopla when promising, not to swear by heaven or God's throne, or by the earth, or by anything. He said this, "Let your 'Yes' be 'Yes,' and your 'No,' 'No'" (v. 37). When Jesus spoke, it was always the truth. When I bend the truth to keep myself out of trouble, then I'm not growing, and worse yet, I am training myself to not even believe what I say and I'm denying Christ's example to us. Now, the call to be honest isn't a free pass to being mean, like saying, "Boy, you look terrible today." That's your opinion, not a fact. But when it comes to confessing why you did something, or owning up to what you've done, or entering into a contract or a commitment, your honesty has to be bigger than your feelings. Your integrity is far too important to waste. Jesus was honest; we should be too.

Spend Some Time

Ever stay up all night? For some, staying up all night is easy. For others, like me, it's not so easy. I like my sleep. In Luke 6:12, the Scripture says, "Jesus went out to a mountainside to pray, and spent the night praying to God." Staying up all night is tough. Staying up and praying is even tougher. There are many instances where Jesus hiked off somewhere to pray. Sometimes, He prayed for a long time. Praying is a cornerstone of our relationship with God and a reminder that our trust is in Him, that there is a hope beyond what we can see with our eyes. In Matthew 6, Jesus told us not to worry about praying long or ornate prayers. He didn't mean we shouldn't spend long periods of time in prayer; He was just telling us not to worry about impressing others. As we can see from Jesus example, it's a good idea to really spend some time in prayer. Jesus prayed all night and that is a long time to pray. The next morning, after spending all that time in prayer, He chose His disciples. Take some time to pray with God today. Pray for others, your leaders, your nation, pray for direction, or just chat with God. Prayer was an important part of Jesus' world changing life. It can be an important part of our lives too.

Encourager

Isn't it a great feeling when someone stops to encourage you? It's a tough world out there, but we know that God is bigger. Jesus has overcome. But in the world, people are being beaten up all day long. Why not be the person today that offers some hope to others? Give an encouraging word to someone. Tell someone they are great and that you value them. Give someone hope and courage to go on. Psalm 10:17 says, "You hear, O LORD, the desire of the afflicted; you encourage them." One thing the afflicted need is a bit of encouragement. And since we are to be imitators of God, we can offer that encouragement. You love the feeling when you're encouraged. Why not be a person who helps others feel that way? Find someone today you can speak real value into. You can say, "Hey, if anyone can win, you can." Spread out the smiles. Encourage your parents, your kids, your siblings, your teachers, coworkers, boss, neighbors, and even that person who just doesn't like you. God is an encourager. We can be too.

Choose to Believe God

Moses led the Israelites to the Promised Land and as they got ready to go in, 12 spies were sent to check out the land. Ten spies came back saying, "No way, we can't go in there," and the other two said, "We can do it. The land is rocking!" All 12 spies saw the same thing, but they had different reactions. We are presented with the same opportunities in life every day. Looking at the same mountain, some will see an obstacle while others will see an opportunity. Those ten spies who said it was impossible to take the land got exactly what they believed. They ended up dying in the wilderness. But the two men who said the land could be taken, Joshua and Caleb, ended up making it to the Promised Land, and both are recorded as heroes in the Bible. Every day we can choose to believe God or to listen to our worries and fears. We can believe God and what He has promised and all that Jesus has achieved, or we can believe the doctors, the newspapers, or we can see the bad instead of the good. God has given His children the land. You are a child of the King. All things are possible with God. There are two choices before you—choose to believe God.

Love Who?!

First John 4:20 says, "For anyone who does not love his brother, whom he has seen, cannot love God, whom he has not seen." Growing up, I can say I didn't always love my brother. It's tough to show love to a brother. The second most important commandment Jesus gave us was to love others. Now, have you ever noticed that we have the hardest time showing our love to those who are closest to us and around the most? The truth is, it's more important to learn to show our love to these than to anyone else. This is the real training ground. I'm talking about learning to really show our love to our spouse, our siblings and our family. This is a great hurdle most of us can work on. Think about it—how can you show your family your love today? Well, love forgives. It doesn't think about its own needs. It forgets all the times people broke stuff and said mean things. Rise above it all. Be more than average in the way you love people. Practice by showing love to those closest to you.

You Are Free

When Jesus came, He proclaimed freedom. Freedom from what? Freedom from a lot of stuff, actually. Psalm 79 says we are now free from death. Hebrews 2:15 says we are even free from the fear of death. Romans 8:21 says we are now free from the bondage of decay and Revelation 1 says we are free from our sinful chains. When Jesus proclaimed freedom for a woman in Luke 13, she was healed. Isaiah 58 says we are free from burdens. Sadly, even though Christ has proclaimed freedom for us, we can still feel a bit tied up, worried, or sick. We can still feel strapped into that bondage of decay, where things seem to be getting worse instead of better. But the truth is, you are free. Jesus said so. In 2 Kings, when Jehoiachin was set free, the Bible says, "So Jehoiachin put aside hisprisonclothesand for the rest of his life ate regularly at the king's table" (2 Kings 25:29). When Jehoiachin was declared free, he took his prison clothes off and put them aside. We need to do the same. You are free. Take off your prison clothes and put them aside. Today, let the worry go. Say goodbye to fear and let the light that God has placed in you light up your world.

Drop Your Doubt

In Matthew 14, Peter was walking on water (which was awesome) but then he started to sink. When this happened, Jesus grabbed him up and said, "You of little faith, why did youdoubt?" (v. 31). Why did Peter start to sink? Well, Jesus said it was because of his doubt. Jesus told His disciples they could wilt fig trees with their words if they did not doubt what they said. Doubt is an enemy in our lives. Now a little doubt might seem harmless, but it's not. When the serpent was tempting Eve to eat the fruit, he started out by saying, "Did God really say not to eat from any tree in the garden?" Satan is the father of lies and a lot of his lies, like this one, are trying to get you to doubt God and what God has said. Doubt can have us eating the wrong fruit or sinking in the water. When we want a mountain out of our way, doubt will leave that mountain staring right back at us. What God has said is true. You are a child of the Most High, created in Christ Jesus to do great things. Let go of doubt.

Your Source

In Luke 13, Jesus proclaimed freedom for a woman and she was healed. Sweet! But He did this on the Sabbath, and one of the synagogue leaders started complaining loudly about Jesus "working" on the Sabbath. Jesus replied, "Should not this woman, a daughter of Abraham, whom Satan has kept bound for eighteen long years, be set free on the Sabbath day from what bound her?" (v. 16). Jesus always had a different answer than others. He spoke differently, prayed differently and saw things differently. Most people just saw a sick woman; Jesus made it a point to say that Satan had bound her. Who bound her? Satan. Who was the source of her pain? Satan. Jesus was willing to put the blame where the blame needed to go. He recognized Satan as the source of the woman's mess, but knew God could be the source of her healing and freedom. We need to know our source. Satan brings death, sin, and destruction, but Satan has been defeated. The source of life, restoration, and healing is Jesus. When Jesus became this woman's source, she was healed. What do you need? Life? Joy? Peace? Wisdom? Well, who is your source? Make God your source.

What Is Your Life Saying?

Where are you going in your life? Are you talking to the wrong people or the right people? Are you up to something you shouldn't be up to? Uh oh. For the most part, we know when we are up to no good. We are hiding our texts messages, erasing the trail so no one knows. Jesus said in Luke 12:57, "Why don't you judge for yourself what is right?" Sometimes we do the right thing because mom or dad or the preacher told us to. That's great, but Jesus takes it deeper. He says, "Hey, it's your life. You judge whether what you're doing is right." You know what? Jesus cares about where you are headed. He's encouraging you to do the right thing. And if doing the right thing were easy, well everyone would be doing it. The truth is that choosing right sets you apart from others. It gets you out of the rut of being average and it removes you from being ordinary. When you choose to do right, your life speaks with a loud voice, "I stand for something, and I am strong enough to stand in what I believe." So where are you going?

Listen to Win

Esther 2:10 says, "Esther had not revealed her nationality and family background, because Mordecia had forbidden her to do so." Mordecai was Esther's uncle who had raised Esther all her life. Esther was now doing what the guy who raised her told her to do. Now, not every kid does what Mom or Dad says. But we see in the story of Esther that her obedience to her uncle who had raised her, though his instruction might seem kind of strange to us, ends up being key to Esther's victory. It saved her life and the lives of thousands in the nation of Israel. Esther could've said, "Hey, I don't have to do what you say," or "I'm not ashamed of where I came from. I'm not hiding." But she didn't; she obeyed Mordecai's instruction. Sometimes those older people who tell us what to do know some things we don't. Sometimes the voice of God plays out through the voices of those who are trying to help us who love us. If Esther hadn't listened and obeyed, she might have lost everything. Who's giving you instructions that just might mean the difference between victory and defeat in your life?

AUGUST 20

It Is Your Job

Have you ever been asked to do something that wasn't your job? Ever been expected to do something that you didn't sign up for? In our world, people are sometimes given a job description and then refuse to do anything outside of that agreement. "Hey, that's not my job. I don't have to do that." But as Christians, we shouldn't have that same attitude. At one point in Jesus' life, He stopped and washed His disciples' feet. Have you ever washed someone's feet? At first, Peter refused to let Jesus wash his feet, saying, "No way, this isn't Your job." I mean think about it, Jesus, the King of kings, anointed one of God, washing the grubby feet of a bunch of dudes. Really? But Jesus showed us a different attitude. Jesus was willing to get His hands dirty. Those feet must have been nasty. Jesus wasn't scared of a little hard work. He showed us that the willingness to do whatever, to serve in whatever way, is the key to being the biggest of leaders. The leader who is willing to get down in the trenches, gains the deepest respect of the people. If Jesus could wash some stinky feet, then so can I.

What Do I Say?

How do I tell others about Christ? This can be an awkward conversation to get into, so many avoid it. Randomly yelling at people who walk by to tell them they are going to hell isn't always effective. In Acts 22, Paul was arrested and as he was being hauled away, he talked the commander into letting him address the crowd that had gathered. When you purpose in your heart to tell the gospel to others, God will make a way, no matter what the circumstance. Paul took this opportunity to preach, and what did he tell them? Did he just tell the story of Christ? No, he told *his* story with Christ. He told them his personal story of how Christ changed him on the road to Damascus. Jesus has changed you. What is your story? People want personal testimony. They want to know how knowing Christ has worked for you. Paul told his story well. He was obviously ready to tell it so that it would be full of impact. Your story is a great one, and it's yours. You tell stories all the time about stuff that has happened to you. So be ready to tell others how you came to know Christ, how it felt, and what changed in your life. God is real, Jesus changed you, and you are real. Now get ready to share!

Heed the Warnings

Paul was on a ship sailing for Rome, when he warned the others with him, "Men, I can see that our voyage is going to be disastrous and bring great loss to ship and cargo, and to our own lives also" (Acts 27:10). But the men sailing with Paul ignored God's warning and sure enough, a storm blew in and destroyed the ship. The men escaped with only their lives. When a storm is in your path of life, listen closely for God's warning. God can help you steer clear of storms. I know sometimes I've looked back on disaster and said, "Oh yeah, I remember when God was trying to steer me around that mess." When tragedy strikes, we sometimes say that God is teaching us something. But maybe the situation wasn't God teaching us something, maybe we just didn't heed the warning He sent. When we find ourselves in the midst of tragedy, we need to remember that God can restore us. But if a person runs a red light and hits another car, maybe rather than try to figure our what God is teaching us in the situation, maybe we should just remember to stop the next time we see a red light.

Watch Your Words

Jesus said that what goes into a man's mouth does not make him unclean; what comes out of his mouth is what makes him unclean. What kind of stuff comes out of your mouth? Do you find yourself saying things like "I hate that guy," or "Did you hear what you- know-who did?" Or do your words sometimes indicate that you expect the worst, like when you say, "Oh, bad stuff always happens to me," or "I'm a moron," or "I can't do it." Maybe what comes out of your mouth isn't the truth, especially when you're trying to come up with an excuse to keep you out of trouble. "Officer, you must be mistaken, I wasn't speeding." Be careful of what you say. The word says that out of the abundance of a man's heart, his mouth speaks. Change your confession - that is, change the way you talk. You may think that you are only describing your circumstances in life, but the truth is, you are creating your circumstances with your words. Instead of saying, "I feel down and depressed," say, "I'm getting happy." If you want things to get better, start by speaking it. Say good things about yourself, your situations, your friends, and your God, and watch your life take a turn for the better.

Following the Rules

It seems like there are rules for everything. There are a million rules we're told to follow from don't drink to don't chew gum in class; from don't murder to don't hate to don't walk on the grass or smoke it. No wonder we keep on sinning! When you think about it, Adam and Eve had it pretty simple. They got to hang out in a perfect garden with God. There was no beer to worry about. It didn't matter how long their hair got because there wasn't a dress code. There was just one simple rule—only one rule. Easy enough, right? The one rule they were given was don't eat of just one particular tree. There were lots of other trees they could eat of, just not that particular one. But even with only one rule to follow, they blew it. Isn't it just like us to want what's forbidden? See, it really doesn't matter how many rules there are, God shows us in this story that it is impossible for man to live without sinning. Only one man ever pulled it off and that was Jesus Christ. He is the Son of God who died for our sins so we can stand righteous before God, despite the fact that we keep messing up. Our job is to believe in Jesus, confess our sins, and know that God is faithful and just to forgive us. Now, we're free to do what Jesus said was important: Love God, and love others.

Fear Not

Ever find yourself playing the "What if" game? What if something goes wrong? What if something bad happens? "What if" is the enemy of our faith in God and our expectation of the fulfillment of God's promises in our lives. "What if" is born in our fears. What are you afraid of? Fear can be very real and gripping. First Peter 5:8 explains that the enemy comes at us like a roaring lion. Now, the job of the roaring lion is to scare you. A group of hunting lions will have the youngest, weakest lion come around roaring and chasing the victim into the trap of the larger lions. The roar is meant to scare and intimidate. The enemy needs you to be afraid in order to have influence in your life. In Judges 14, Samson was attacked by a young roaring lion. But instead of being frightened and running, Samson faced the lion. The Spirit of the Lord came upon Samson in power so that he tore the lion apart. Now, I'm not asking you to go and fight with lions, but when fear tries to grip you and take a place in your life, don't give it control. Face that lion and expect God to give you the power you need to rip it all apart. Fear attempts to tell you how you should feel, and it tries to influence your decisions. Don't give in that kind of influence in your life!

Denial and Crosses

Let me break something to you: It's not about you. How many churches split and how many families leave the church because the pastor offended them or because the music was too loud? Jesus says in Luke chapter 9 that we must deny ourselves, take up our cross and follow Him. But what does that mean? First, let's understand what it means to deny ourselves. I'll refer to music again, for obvious reasons. It really doesn't matter if you like the style of music your church does for praise and worship. Stop and realize that maybe that style of music is for someone else. Someone else will be deeply ministered to by the very music you don't like. You can accomplish so much more for God when you stop being concerned about how everything affects you. Next, let's understand what it means to take up our cross. What is our cross? The cross was Jesus' destiny. It was the fulfillment of His earthly commission. Our cross is whatever plan, purpose and ministry God has given us. So, the message Jesus is trying to give us is quite simple. We need to get over ourselves and follow God to our destiny. Now that you have your instructions, why not get started today?

Voice Mail

Sometimes I really hate getting people's voice mail. You know what I mean? You call a number, and instead of getting to talk to the person you needed to talk to, a voice you've never heard before tells you, "I'm sorry, but the person you called is unavailable. To page this person, press one. To leave a message, stay on the line. After you are finished recording your message, press pound for more options." It's bad enough that you don't get to talk to your friend, but it's even worse that your friend didn't take the time to set up their voice mail, so you get the automated voice, not a personal message from your friend. It probably seems pretty random to be talking about voice mail messages, but the point I want you to take is that you never know what might make an impact on someone. Even in little things, like the message people get when they call your voice mail, we need to be looking for ways to encourage others or make their lives better. The Bible tells us to make the most of every opportunity. Who knew that would include voice mail, too?

Real Help

I was performing a magic trick the other day. Now, I'm not much of a magician, but the trick went well and I fooled everyone. People like to watch magic tricks. What's happening is not real magic; it's a trick. Now, why am I talking about magic? Sometimes we wish we could use magic to solve our problems in life, don't we? We think that maybe if we could just find a genie in a bottle, then we would own the world. But what we need is not magic, we need what God calls miracles, which are not a tricks, they're real. Jesus said in Mark 11:24, "Whatever you ask for in prayer, believe that you have received it, and it will be yours." God wants us to be successful and full of joy. So what do you need to achieve this in your life? You may have asked everyone you know for help, but have you asked God? If you've asked, then believe! Sometimes I need a little help in my life along the way, and when I remember to pray and include God in my problems, He shows up. He always has a better solution than I do. James 4:2 teaches that we do not have because we do not ask God. What do you need? A job? A car? How about your friends, what do they need? Pray for them. God will help, and His help isn't magic and it's not make believe.

Be Careful What You Plant

I planted grass in my yard once. When I went to the store to buy the seed, I noticed there were twenty-five pound bags of seed for $5, or I could buy five pound bags of seed for $25. Well, I bought the cheap seed. What I didn't know was that the cheaper grass seed wasn't actually grass seed, but it was weed seed with some grass seed mixed in. When the seed took root, the soil in my yard didn't know to only grow the grass. It grew everything I planted, weeds as well. Proverbs 4:23 says to guard your heart with all diligence, for it is the wellspring of life. The heart is like my yard. Whatever you let get planted in your heart will grow. What you think and what you say are seeds that grow desire in your heart. If you think about wrong things, you will grow desire to do those wrong things. If you think about someone who was mean to you, you'll get mad at them. Desire demands action. Have you ever spent a bunch of time thinking about a car that you like? Soon you feel like you have to have it, and you will try and figure out a way to buy it. A desire for a car isn't wrong, but be careful what you plant in your heart. Make sure your thoughts and words are planting the right desires in your heart so that you can lead a happy life.

Fine Workmanship

Ephesians 2:10 tells us that we are God's workmanship, created in Christ Jesus to do good works which God prepared in advance for us to do. God doesn't make junk and we are God's workmanship. He makes good stuff. Remember, as God created the heavens and the earth, He would finish each day by looking around and saying, "It is good." You are good. A wise man once pointed out that a poor self-esteem is an insult to the Creator. So as you look at the outside and the inside of yourself, you should think, *Hey good job, God.* But as you look at yourself, don't get conceited. You also need to realize that God created you so perfectly in Christ Jesus because He has good works for you to do. There is some stuff God needs for you to do for Him. Lots of Christians wait around for God to do everything, but God prepared stuff for us to do. Every day, you are presented with a new set of hours in which to accomplish something. Who are you going to work for today? The devil? Yourself? God? Who you work for matters. Fulfill your destiny today - dig into the good works you've been created to do.

What He Did With All They Had

The crowd Jesus had been teaching was hungry and it was getting late, so Jesus told His disciples to feed the group. Well, there were 5000 men, plus women and children. The disciples were overwhelmed by the task. Did you know that God also has very big things for you to do? He has prepared in advance tasks for you to do that are too big for you. Does that scare you? Remember that after Jesus told His disciples to feed the group, He then asked the disciples, "What do you have?" They had five loaves of bread and two fish. Doesn't seem like nearly enough, does it? But do you remember what happened when the disciples gave everything they had to Jesus? Everyone was fed with plenty of food left over. Jesus wants you to use everything you have to accomplish the task in front of you. If you will use all you have, God will do the rest. In fact, God will make what you have more than enough. But you have to step out, choose to believe God, and take on that impossible dream with vigor. Give God your all.

SEPTEMBER 1

One Last Thing Before Sleep

There's a list of things I do when it's time to go to sleep: set the alarm clock, turn off the lights, charge the phone, turn off the TV... let's see, what am I forgetting? Well there may be something more important than making sure there is a glass of water on my bedside table and all my good nights have been said. Ephesians 4:26 says, "'In your anger do not sin': Do not let the sun go down while you are still angry." Notice that anger itself is not a sin. But here, we find out it can become sin if we fall asleep while angry. God knows how we are built. He made us and He knows if we don't let our anger go, then it can get rooted deep in our heart. Sure, we may wake up feeling fine. We may even have forgotten about our anger, but it's still in there, deep in your heart, just waiting to ooze out as something terrible. So, before the sun sets on your day, let go of your anger and forgive.

Praise Before the Harvest

Have you ever worked and worked and worked, but it just didn't seem to amount to anything? Well, one of the results of Adam's sin was that God told him that as he worked, the earth would no longer produce for him. Thorns and thistles would be all he would get. Psalm 67 teaches us a way to overcome this curse, though. It says in verses 5-6, "May the people praise you, oh God…Then the land will yield its harvest." We want our work to reap a harvest. We want our work to produce and make a difference and be successful. But the fact is, most of us think of praising God *after* the big blessing comes in. Here, God shows us His plan. He says that we should praise Him first. Then, after the praising, the harvest comes in. God wants to be thanked even before we see the blessing or the victory. Do you know why He would share this secret with us? It's because He's excited to see us win, He's excited for our harvest. He wants us to succeed. Even before the harvest comes in, to God be the glory!

Need Answers?

I love watching a movie where the hero is out of ideas, out of strength, and then just when you think the hero is ready to give up, he realizes the secret to winning the battle. He finds some clue he needs to turn it all around. Really, in any test whether at school or life, the only way to pass is to know the answers. Jeremiah 33:3 says, "Call to me and I will answer you and tell you great and unsearchable things you do not know." So, imagine you are the hero of your movie, and here you're told where to access the answers you need to win. What do you do? How do you get the answers? It's simple—call to God. So often we spend all our time trying to reason and think it all through to find the best answer, making a list of pros and cons. Should I move? Should I quit? Where should I go to college? Is she the right one for me? Big life questions deserve a real life God, and He isn't even far away. Trade in a bit of brain time for praying time. Call to God. He knows a bunch of stuff that you don't and He's waiting to share the answers with you.

Leave the Nets

Transition is the movement from one area to another. Think of it as moving to another home. Living in one home is fine, and living in the next home is fine. But the moving part is a lot of work. Transition usually consists of a short period of intense work, and the more baggage you bring through transition, the harder the transition becomes. In Matthew 4:19, Jesus approached some fishermen and said, "Come, follow Me, and I will make you fishers of men." At once, these men left their nets and followed Him. Notice two things, they did not hesitate, and they left their nets behind. Leaving their nets behind meant that there could be no going back to that old way of life. They were done with the nets. When we choose to follow Christ, we too need to let go of our old way of life, our old nets, our old thinking. The more we try and bring with us, the harder it will become to follow Him. If your nets are keeping you in the past, well put them down, make the transition, and start brand new today.

The Whole Truth

Did you know that the media doesn't always give you the whole truth and what others tell you may not be exactly correct, either? It's important that before we make judgments, we understand the full truth for ourselves. In John 6:53, Jesus said to the crowd, "I tell you the truth, unless you eat the flesh of the Son of Man and drink his blood, you have no life in you." When a lot of Christ's followers heard this, they were freaked out by what Jesus said, so they deserted Him. Looking back now, boy did they miss out. *They walked away from the Son of God!* But how many of us have chosen to walk away from the truth of God because of misunderstandings? Jesus is the way, the truth, and the life. His words are true. These followers had simply misunderstood what He was saying. We need to press into God's Word to discover the truth for ourselves so we don't miss out, allowing ourselves to be led the wrong way.

Go Tell that Fox

One day, Jesus was out teaching and healing when some Pharisees came by and told Him that He'd better leave or Herod, the leader of that region, was going to have Him killed. In Luke 13:32 Jesus replied, "Go tell that fox, 'I will drive out demons and heal people today and tomorrow, and on the third day I will reach my goal.'" Jesus showed that He was immoveable from what He had decided to do and no threat was going to change that. He had a goal—a big goal of dying for the sins of the world. Jesus described His goal as something He was going to reach. The very idea of reaching for something implies it may be a stretch to attain. Jesus' goal was to help others. Notice that this interruption from the Pharisees didn't distract him from His goal. When we set goals that we have to reach for, goals to help others, we need to remember that obstacles, distractions, or even mountains may come our way and try to stop us. When a mountain comes your way, remember Jesus' words, "Go tell that fox…that I will reach my goal." And you will!

Do the Right Thing

Nothing starts a day off better than orange juice all down the front of my shirt. You may think it's no big deal, but it was a white shirt, and new, and I really liked it. I could have just thrown on an orange tie to match the stain. But instead, I began washing it, trying to get the stain out. When the stain wasn't coming out, I switched products, scrubbed harder, and tried my very best to get my shirt spotless. Second Peter 3:14 says, "...make every effort to be found spotless." Here's some good news—when you believe in Christ as the Son of God, His blood washes you and makes you spotless. That's right! Before we knew Christ, sin had stained us. Now through Christ, we have experienced the best stain remover of all times. You are now white as snow. So don't be confused when this Scripture tells us to make an effort to be spotless. It is by grace we are saved, not by how good we are. But God wants us to make an effort to do the right thing. In fact, we should make every effort to do right, to be honest, faithful, giving, loving, to serve and help others. Give to God and serve the body of Christ. Make every effort to do the right thing because of what Christ has done for us.

Credit for the Win

Whatever you are doing today, be great at it. Let your trying, your perseverance, your refusal to give up be part of who you are. You are capable of greatness. God created you that way. So when you accomplish great things, talk about God. When you score that goal, ace that test, or win that contract, or when you help carry someone's load, encourage another to win, or buy some shoes for a kid who needs them, give the glory to God. The Word teaches us to not go advertising our goodness, just be good. Let your actions speak for themselves. Proverbs 27:2 says, "Let another praise you and not your own mouth." Save your words for encouraging and cheering on others. There's no need to toot your own horn. When you hit the game winning shot, give credit to the team for winning, not just you. The truth is that when you are a child of the King, you are going to win big. When you do, send the glory to God and encourage others.

See Like God Sees

How do you see yourself? Do you see yourself as God sees you? If not, whose opinion do you think is right? Proverbs 27:21 says that, "Man is tested by the praise he receives." Why would praise test you? Well, when someone says, "Hey you're really smart," while deep within your heart, you think you're not smart, your opinion will begin to war with the praise. It's a test. Or maybe someone says, "You look pretty," but you actually think you're ugly, then a fight begins within you as you think, *No, I'm not pretty.* If you deal with feelings of worthlessness, but you begin to be successful, you risk thwarting that success as you make your life reflect what you truly think of yourself. You may start to lose on purpose so that your life will look like how you feel inside. God wants you to know that you are a smart, beautiful, wonderful creation; that you have the mind of Christ, you are a child of the King, and He is crowning you with glory, blessing you in every way, and has equipped you to win as a light in this world. God sees you as wonderful and you should too!

The Eyes Lie

Proverbs 27:20 says, "Death and Destruction are never satisfied, and neither are the eyes of man." What are you looking at? Our eyes are capable of always seeing something. We want more than what we have. For this reason, our eyes cannot be satisfied. And when you are not satisfied, well, you're not happy. God has a better plan. He tells us to walk by faith and not by sight. Our faith is satisfied by the Lord. Fulfillment can only come from God, whom we cannot see. Your eyes might try to find someone better looking than the person you're with, a nicer car than the one you're driving, a better suit, a bigger house, more, more, more! If you let your eyes lead, they will take you to death and destruction—to always feeling like you don't have what you want. Instead of thinking of what you want, ask yourself what God wants. He wants to grow the local church, which is the body of Christ, and to get His Word out. He wants for you to give, serve, and love Him *and* others. Your eyes will lie to you. Seeing isn't always believing. Close your eyes and follow God.

Zephaniah's Truth

Have you ever been in mess when you looked to heaven and asked, "Well, where's God?" I've got great news—Zephaniah 3:17 says, "The Lord your God is with you." Yep, He's right here. Just because you can't see Him doesn't mean He's not around. You might be thinking that even though He's here, maybe He's not interested in helping you. But, that's not true either. This verse goes on to say, "He is mighty to save." Okay, you'll buy that, but then you might say, "Well, I think He's mad at me today." The verse answers that assumption, too: "He will take great delight in you." That is like saying God really loves you, that you make Him smile. The verse finishes by saying, "He will quiet you with His love, He will rejoice over you with singing." God is with you. He wants to help you. He loves you and just hanging out with you makes Him want to sing about you. Imagine God rejoicing over you with singing. The world may not want you to win, and the enemy may do what he can to stop you, but God is definitely with you every step of the way.

Speak the Word

When Jesus healed, He never spoke the problem; He spoke the solution. *Eyes, open. Lame, get up and walk. Leprosy, be clean.* He told the problem what it needed to do instead of describing the gloom. Remember when the storm was raging on? Jesus rebuked it and said, "Peace, be still." As followers of Christ, this is an example for us. When we talk about the problem, it makes us feel worse. Isaiah 8:20-21 says it like this, "If they do not speak according to this word, they have no light of dawn. Distressed and hungry, they will roam through the land." This passage goes on to say that all of the stress and hunger will cause them to curse the king and God. We don't ever want to be so worked up that we get mad at God. Look at what the Word tells us to do. It says to speak according to the Word (meaning the Bible). Well then, what does the Bible say? It says you are more than a conqueror in Christ Jesus, that you are the head and not the tail, above and not beneath, blessed coming in and blessed going out. Speak that kind of stuff! Obey God with your mouth and watch your situation change.

You've Got to Sow

Ecclesiastes 11:2 says, "Give portions to seven, yes to eight, for you do not know what disaster may come upon the land." This verse is telling us to think about what we can give while we have something to give. When we think of disaster, we may think, "I better hold on to everything I have in case things get worse." God has a different plan. He says to be a giver when you can. He considers it sowing seed and the idea is this: Sowing will always result in more. The passage goes on to say "Whoever watches the wind will not plant; whoever looks at the clouds will not reap" (v. 4). The reaping comes only after a planting. We want the harvest, but God is showing us that if we are so busy watching for wind or clouds, keeping our eyes in a place of worry like the finance section of the newspaper, it will keep us from planting. Worrying about the future will keep us from planting and if we don't plant, then we will not reap. Instead of worrying, remember that God is your source. It is He who has given you the ability to gain wealth, thereby confirming His covenant with you.

IMPORTANT ANNOUNCEMENT!

Young people listen up! If you plan to get married one day, then you need to know that who you marry is one of the most important decisions you will *ever make*. Let me ask you a question. Is the world's system for marriage working? No, it isn't. The world's ideas for dating and marriage are broken. The system has failed. God's system for marriage works wonderfully. God designed the very first marriage when He created Adam and Eve, and at that time, the divorce rate was 0%. That marriage lasted. I would guess Adam and Eve were married hundreds of years. That's a long time to make it work. Most Americans can't stay married past 15 years. So who shouldn't you marry? When Jacob was going to go find a wife, his mom and dad said, "Do not marry a Canaanite woman." A Canaanite was symbolic of the world, so what Jacob's parents were telling him was don't marry a *worldly* girl. It doesn't matter how good looking or fun that person is, worldly is worldly and you know **exactly** what I mean by that! Pray for your future spouse and follow God's plan. Look for a mate who fears God and who is strong in moral character. This is someone who will love you for a lifetime.

Firsthand Knowledge

In Genesis 28, we find Jacob as he has just moved out of his parents' home. His first night away from home, God gave him a dream. He woke up and said, "Surely the Lord is in this place, and I was not aware of it" (v. 16). I've got news for you—even when you leave home, God is still around. Okay, get ready for this: God is *everywhere*. You can try and run from Him or you can seek Him like you should, but eventually you will feel His presence deep in your heart. Until this time, maybe Jacob saw God as someone his mom and dad knew, or even someone they invented. That night, Jacob found out about God firsthand. He was faced with believing in God for himself. As you get older, you have to determine what you believe. It may be time to crack open that Bible or fall to your knees and find God for yourself. Find out who He is, what He says, what He does, what He doesn't do, why He sent His Son, who His Son is, and what He represents. Lots of people will tell you what they believe about God, but what do you believe? Seek Him in His sanctuary, pray, open your Bible and learn. It's time!

Coming Home

Jeremiah 2:13 says, "My people have committed two sins: They have forsaken me, the spring of living water, and have dug their own cisterns, broken cisterns that cannot hold water." You know, it isn't a new thing that sometimes God's people walk away from Him. People try and do life on their own or think they have a better idea. Or maybe they get discouraged, or decide that the pleasures of the world are more fun. But eventually, they find out that without Jesus, the cistern in them runs dry. This may be you. You knew God, but you walked away for this reason or that. Truth is, you're not a bad person. You are in a world that has a lot of wrong thinking and it can be hard to come out of that. But it is not by accident that you are reading this today. The well within you is running dry, but Jesus has a spring of living water for you. God has called you to come home. Sometimes the people of God forsake God, but remember that God will never forsake you. The blood of Jesus has reconciled you to God. Right now, you can have a brand new beginning with God. Tell God right now, "Lord, forgive me. I hear You calling, and I'm coming home."

New Thing? Nah.

Back in the old days when I was a kid, the only phone in our house was plugged into a wall. Remember those things? There was no cell phone, texting, or voice mail. You couldn't walk very far when you were on the phone, because of the wire that attached to the wall. The cord would get all tangled up into a ball from people twirling it, and it wasn't just one person's phone—you shared it with your whole household. When the phone rang, you answered it, not knowing who was calling or whom they were calling for. If you were waiting on someone to call you and your brother was on the phone, well forget it. Thank goodness those days are over. See, new stuff comes out all the time and changes how we think and how we live. But you know who doesn't change? God. He's the same yesterday, today and forever. For 2,000 years, the message of Christ in the Bible has spoken life to anyone who would listen, regardless of the technology, culture, or era they lived in. People think that the next new thing will improve our life, save us time, or make things easier, but really what we need is still the same no matter when you live. We need Jesus.

A Light for the Search

If you're looking for something at night, what do you need? A light, right? And if you're searching, the more light the better. John 1 tells us that Jesus is the Word of God and He is light. The Word of God, or the Bible, is described as a *lamp unto my feet*. Now listen to this— Proverbs 20:27 says, "The lamp of the Lord searches the spirit of a man, it searches out his inmost being." So what is going on in your inmost being? You may not be sure, but I think it would be good to know since your innermost being is you. Now, lots of people try and search for themselves, trying to find out who they really are. But who you really are can only be revealed by the One who created you, and the tool He uses to make this revelation is the Bible. It is the lamp you need to discover who you really are, what you can really do, what you are capable of, what you really want, or what you are here to do. What is your purpose? That's a good question, and as you search for the answer, make sure you grab your light—the Bible.

Your Assignment

After Jesus rose from the dead He ascended to the heavens, but first, He left His disciples with an assignment. What was that assignment? What did the disciples do? I mean, what did they dedicate the rest of their days on earth to doing? When Paul joined in to help, what was he helping with? What was Peter doing? What was the purpose of the letters the apostles wrote and who were they written for? The disciples of Jesus were all doing the same thing. Each of them was planting churches, growing churches, writing letters to churches, training up leaders of churches, teaching in the churches, and telling people about Jesus. As people were saved, they would organize them into a church. This is the assignment Jesus left for His disciples to do. These were great men of God who were carrying out their assignment. You also can carry this torch. We can learn from the early apostles and gain focus of what to do today and tomorrow. Let's grow the local church. It's the body of Christ and even the bride of Christ. Think today... what can you do to help grow your church and carry out the assignment Jesus gave all of us?

Good Medicine

Proverbs 17:22 says, "A cheerful heart is good medicine." When do you need medicine? Isn't it when you aren't feeling good? Maybe you have a headache or a stuffy nose. *I can't stand a stuffy nose.* Medicine is a fix for an ailment. But what about when your heart is feeling sick, down or broken? Here, the scripture doesn't describe what sickness a cheerful heart is good medicine for, so I think God is saying that it is good medicine for whatever is going on. But how can you have a cheerful heart when you're not feeling good? I mean, the overall idea of not feeling good is very anti-cheerful. God is showing us that a cheerful heart is something you choose, not because you feel like it, but because you know it's the right thing to do. Have you ever noticed that medicine usually tastes nasty? Well, choosing to have a cheerful heart might be the same. What I mean is, when you are down, the last thing you want is to take some cheery heart as medicine. So, how are you feeling? Do you need some medicine? Well, put the Pepto away, plug your nose, and drink a hot cup of cheery heart. It goes down rough, but you'll be feeling happy in no time. Now take your medicine!

Say You're Sorry

The art of apologies has been lost in our society. Have you ever messed up and hurt someone's feelings or accidentally bumped into someone? Did you say you were sorry? A lot of times, people just sweep stuff under the rug instead of asking someone to forgive them. Being sorry is powerful when you mess up. And we will all mess up. Let's say your parents are really on you about your grades. You could get mad and slam the door. But what if you looked at them both and out of your mouth came these words, "You know what, I'm trying, but maybe I could try harder. I know you are upset because you care about my future. I'm sorry. Will you forgive me?" Wow. In our society, it is a rare thing for someone to say they are sorry. In Matthew 4:17, the Scriptures tells us that, "From that time on Jesus began to preach, 'Repent, for the kingdom of heaven is near.'" Repentance is saying sorry to God and then turning away from bad behavior. Have you ever done something that was wrong, even if by accident? Well sure, we all have. Tell God you are sorry. He is faithful and just to forgive you of your sins. Jesus came to earth, died and rose from the dead to bring reconciliation between man and God. Some people wallow in guilt or make excuses or get really angry when they mess up. But Jesus has a better way—just repent. Say, "Father God, I messed up. Please forgive me." And He will.

Why Church?

An ABC poll released in March of 2009 said that about 50% of Christians attend church regularly. So I guess of the people reading this, about half of you don't go to church. Why go to church? I mean, it's not a big deal, is it? I found it strange that at one time, life insurance companies asked prospective policyholders if they attended church regularly. I wanted to find out why this question was on their applications. Life insurance companies track statistics very closely and accurately as part of being in the business of betting on the life of a person. Here is what I found. It is a fact that people who attend church regularly are less likely to develop cancer, heart disease and mental illness. Teens who attend church are four times less likely to commit suicide. People who attend church will spend, on average, half as much time in the hospital. They are five times less likely to need antibiotics, they have significantly lower blood pressure, and they live, on average, seven years longer than those who do not attend church. People who attend church regularly report a 50% higher average annual income and have a substantially lower number of heart attacks than do non-churchgoers. The cities with highest church attendance report the lowest crime rates in the nation. Church attendance is the number one predictor of marital stability. Married couples who report attending church regularly and one marriage seminar per year report less than a 1% divorce rate. (All statistics were taken from 2008 reports from Insurance Statistics, Duke University, Demography, The American Medical News, and the National Institute of Health Care Research in America.) Hebrews 10:25 tells us to not forsake gathering together, as many are in the habit of doing. Make a decision to find a good church today and make a commitment to attend.

Servants

In Mark 10:45, Jesus said, "For even the Son of Man did not come to beserved, but toserve, and to give his life as a ransom for many." The King of kings was telling us all that He came to serve. Learning to be a great leader always starts with service. If you can help someone else be great, then God will promote you. Look at Joshua, who served as Moses' aide for 40 years. Think about David, who served King Saul in battle and as a musician. Who remembers Elisha, who served the great prophet Elijah? In each of these cases, the servant eventually went beyond the leader. Joseph started out as a slave, and Nehemiah was cupbearer to the king. When we serve, we learn to be just, to think of others, and we learn what it is like to work hard for the man. We can bring these lessons with us when we lead, so that we will value people and remember the importance of serving, even as a leader. Not sure how to get involved in service? Well, I encourage you to help out at church. Join the ushers or greeters or prayer ministry. Help teach kids in the Sunday school class. Serve. And when you work your job or help a customer, remember to serve with your whole heart. It is Christ who reminds us that if we can be faithful with the little things, then will He make us rulers over much (Matthew 25:23).

Giving Thanks

First Chronicles 16:34 says, "Give thanks to the LORD, for He is good; his love endures forever." That sounds like a worship song. Notice that *thanks* is something you give. That may have meant more 3,000 years ago than it does today. Today, we give thanks by saying, "Thank you." But 3,000 years ago, giving thanks meant words accompanied by a gift. You would quite literally "give" thanks. In fact, there was a specific offering the people would bring to the temple of the Lord called the thanksgiving offering. Their thanks included a gift. The offering went to the temple, but the thanks went to the Lord. Today, we have much to be thankful for. You might say, "Well no, not me. I'm in a real bad way right now." But really, we can always find a reason to be thankful, even if it is just thanking God that the sun came up again. We can thank God for the air we breathe and the food we eat. But when you think of thanking God, what can you give? The widow gave just a mite. It was all she had and Jesus stood up and honored her for it. When the offering is received at your church, take up a special gift above your tithes and offer it to the Lord with a heart of thankfulness. You cannot out give God. When you offer thanks with your gift, who knows what could happen. A little boy once brought a few loaves and fish to Jesus. The scripture says in Mark 14:22 that Jesus took the bread, gave thanks and broke it. You know there wasn't enough in that little boy's lunch to feed all those people, but that small gift combined with thanks fed a multitude. It can happen for you!

Who Are You Hanging With?

Are your friends eagles or beagles? That's more than just a great rhyme—choosing those you hang around is very important. Jesus didn't hang around just anyone. He specifically handpicked His disciples. He didn't just pass out a disciple sign-up sheet or randomly run into a nice guy in a pub and ask if he wanted to join the band. In the Bible, there are accounts of people asking if they could follow Jesus, and Jesus would say no. Really. A man who had been demon possessed wanted to leave with Christ, but Jesus instructed him to stay in his town and fix the mess he had caused. Some have said that Jesus' friends were the sinners and drunks—that is what the Pharisees said. But the people who were His close companions, who went from town to town with Him, were not the sinners He preached to; they were His disciples. Now what about you? Are you choosy with friends? Are your friends building you up or dragging you down? Are you always having to encourage and rescue your friends? Are they following God? If not, do you find they influence you sometimes? Are your friends rooting you on to success or are they comfortable with you being average? Being around the right people can really change your expectations in life. Get around others who love God and are really going somewhere, and you will be amazed how much more inspired you will become.

Equipment

Imagine a football player taking the defensive line without wearing pads. (Ouch.) Or, imagine a soldier taking the battlefield without a weapon. (Dude, where's your sword?) To be successful, we need the right equipment for the job we are doing. In life, God is equipping you for success. You have been built to win. In 2 Timothy 3:16-17, God says, "All Scripture is God-breathed and is useful for teaching, rebuking, correcting and training in righteousness,so that the man of God may be thoroughly equipped for every good work." When you accepted Jesus, you became the man or woman of God; now God's Word will thoroughly equip you to do that job. God's equipment is good; it's the best you can get. God is not equipping you to fail. His equipment is built for glorious victory. And when God equips you, you know you're thoroughly equipped! Are you ready to win today? When you are equipped with God's Word, you win! So, go get em!

Take Off Your Shoes and Be Holy

God called to Moses out of a burning bush and said, "Moses…take off your sandals, for the place where you are standing is holy ground" (Exodus 3:5). What was so special about that ground that it was holy? If you read on through the Bible, you will find many instances where God tells us that whatever touches something that is holy will become holy. So that's what made that ground holy—Holy God was in that place. So why did God tell Moses to take off his shoes? I think it's because He knew that when Moses' feet touched the holy ground, he would become holy. Holy means to be set apart for God's plans. The awesome news is that you, too, have been made holy! When you received Christ, you were washed in His blood, which is holy. That makes you holy. When Moses took off his shoes, it was like he was taking off his past. His shoes represented everywhere he had been up until that moment. God is not concerned with our past, but with our future. We must let go of our past to start something new. The blood of Jesus washes away our past. You are now set apart for God's plans. Are you ready? Great, here we go!

Beating Temptation

On the night that He was betrayed, Jesus was praying in the Garden of Gethsemane and His disciples fell asleep. He woke them up and said, "Watch and pray so that you will not fall into temptation. The spirit is willing, but the body is weak" (Matthew 26:41). I think we can all agree the body is weak. It doesn't always want good stuff and it can be pretty demanding. And being a Christian doesn't mean we automatically stop falling into temptation. So Jesus gives us a hint about beating temptation. Jesus said to watch and pray so that we won't fall into temptation. So when temptation comes your way, try a little watching and a little praying. You could say in your prayer, "Woah, oh, Lord, I could use a little help here and some strength because I'm being tempted." Our natural reaction during temptation is to hide our sin, but Jesus is telling us to pray, talk to God, and allow Him to help. You could say, "Father, my spirit knows what to do, but my body is weak; it wants to do something else. I could use You about now." Imagine how amazing life would be if every time temptation came your way, it reminded you to pray. That would get us all praying a bit more, and that has to be good.

Loving Others

Psalm 48:9 says, "Within your temple, O God, we meditate on your unfailing love." The greatest commandments that Jesus gave us were all about love. The world teaches one kind of love, but God teaches us a different kind. For instance, God's love remembers no wrongs, but I sometimes keep a record of wrongs. This just means I have some more learning to do. This verse says that it is in the temple where we meditate on God's love. So God is saying that a great place to meditate on love is in His house, which is the church. It's a great place to think about how we can love better, to listen and learn about love, and to practice loving. Since love requires others, church is a great place to do it. There are other people around with whom you can exercise love at church. Sadly, some people quit church because someone wasn't being very loving to them. That's sad because that's exactly why we are there—to love. Being a Christian sometimes means learning how to love others who aren't all that loveable. Or maybe you're the one who is hard to love! Either way, go to church, get around some people and learn to love the way God loves.

Promises, Promises

Psalm 119:50 says, "My comfort in my suffering is this: Your promise preserves my life." Sometimes days don't go so great. It's a weird and often abusive world with a real enemy trying to get you down. But in this verse, we find out that God has a comfort available to us. It is His promise, which preserves our life. Now, life is good. It's about more than just surviving. To be alive is to be preserved by God's promise. What is this promise? Is it that things are going to get worse? Well no, because if the promise is that things will get worse, then that wouldn't be a very good comfort. The promise must be one of hope. A promise that preserves life is one that says things are going to get better. Second Peter 1:4 refers to God's promises as great and precious. Now, if I came up to you and said I wanted to make a very great and precious promise to you, you'd probably get excited. You'd be expecting something really good. Well, get excited because God wants you to be comforted knowing that He's got great promises for you.

The Right Choice

A Twinkie or broccoli? Tell the truth and get in trouble or tell a lie and maybe get away with it? Do what Mom or Dad says or don't? Homework or TV? Make fun of the goofy kid or defend the goofy kid? Decisions, decisions, decisions. In Genesis 2:8, it says that in the middle of the Garden of Eden were the tree of life *and* the tree of the knowledge of good and evil. God gave one rule to Adam and Eve—no eating from the tree of the knowledge of good and evil. There was plenty of other good stuff to eat—in fact, right near the forbidden tree was the tree of life! From the very beginning, God gave man a decision to make. We can listen to the serpent, calling from the wrong tree, "Hey, over here. This is the good fruit. It'll be fine. Mom or Dad will never know." But this is your life we're talking about—maybe you should choose the right tree. I mean, Adam and Eve picked the wrong tree, but you don't have to. You can choose the Tree of Life rather than the other tree. Make the right choice.

World Change

In Exodus 5, Moses and Aaron were telling Pharaoh that God wanted him to let the Israelites go, but Pharaoh said, "Who is the LORD, that I should obey him and let Israel go? I do not know the LORD..." (v. 2). You see, the world will not listen to God until they know God. Sometimes we get upset with people in the world because they don't do things the way we think they should. Sometimes we even get all blogging and hating about it. We shouldn't be surprised that the world publishes books, magazines, and web pages, or opens companies or makes decisions that we think are wrong. Our fight isn't with what they are doing; our battle is for the heart of the person. Changing the world won't happen by us telling people they are messed up sinners. Instead, we should start by introducing the person to God. Let God change them. Let forgiveness and compassion reign in your heart. Love others and genuinely want them to have a relationship with the Father. Jesus said that if you know Him, then you also know the Father. Introduce others to Jesus, His message, His love, His death, and His resurrection. Tell them about the hope Christ brought you. People are dying out there. You can help change this world. Introduce someone to Christ today.

Plenty of Grapes

What is God like? What does He want for us? Learning about God and His desire for you is as simple as reading the Bible. Sometimes I hear people say, "Well, I just am not sure what God wants for me." That may be true, but you don't have to "not know," because God provided the answers for us in the Word. Here is a scripture from the Old Testament that gives us just a small snapshot into how God desires for us to live. Leviticus 26:4-5 says, "I will send you rain in its season, and the ground will yield its crops and the trees of the field their fruit. Your threshing will continue until grape harvest and the grape harvest will continue until planting, and you will eat all the food you want and live in safety in your land." Wow, that passage tells us a lot about God. We see that God wants us to be blessed, to get rain when it is supposed to rain, make sure the work we do produces, that we have fruit—apparently more grapes than a person could ever need—to eat all the food we want (healthy food, I'm sure), and to be safe. Could you use these things? Yes? Well praise God, here they come!

How Much Can You See?

When God was giving the Israelites the Promised Land, He told them in Numbers 34 what the boundaries of their land would be. So, where did these boundaries come from? I mean, why have these boundaries? It all may have started back in Genesis 13 when Abraham was in the Promised Land 440 years earlier. God says in Genesis 13:14-15, "Lift up your eyes from where you are and look north and south, east and west. All the land that you see I will give to you and your offspring forever." How much land was Abraham promised? Well, it was all of the land that he could see. Now the Promised Land is far too big for him to have been able to see it all, so Abraham was seeing beyond what his natural eyes showed him. Jesus lived a limitless life every day because He could see what we cannot. Let's learn from this today and allow God to begin to enlarge what we can see. What can God do in your life? Can He change your tomorrow? Does prayer still get answered? Can miracles still happen? Today, let's all begin to see bigger!

Excel

First Corinthians 14:12 says, "Try to excel in gifts that build up the church." There are a few things for us to consider from this verse. First is the effort. We should be trying. Trying to what? Well, trying to excel, which means to be excellent. Maybe you aren't excellent yet, but according to this, you should try. Ok, so we should try to be excellent... at what? This verse tell us to be excellent in gifts that build the church. There are three types of people I see around me. First, I see some who are trying to excel in gifts to build up the church. Second, I see some who are just attending church. And third, I see others who are actually trying to tear down the church. The world trains us to either not go to church, or if we're going to go, the world tells us to attack the church. But God has a different message for us. God tells us to give our best effort to do something really great that builds the church. This may mean changing how we think about church, but isn't that just like the Bible, always growing us up? You see, church is not about what I'm getting, but it's about what I'm giving. If we all got busy building the church in excellence, just think about what could happen.

Truth Is Truth

First Timothy 3:2 says, "Now the overseer must be above reproach, the husband of but one wife." Whoa, hold on there. What did he just say? The overseer must have just one wife. Well, that's good advice for a lot of reasons. You know, sometimes people get the idea that the Bible is okay with someone having a bunch of wives. Now, I doubt anyone reading this is thinking about getting a second or third wife. I only bring this subject up because I don't like it when people get the wrong idea about what the Bible teaches. People might say, "Well the Bible says Solomon had 700 wives." Sure, but was that God's plan for him? Nope. And those wives got him in a heap of trouble. He began to worship other gods because of his many wives. The Bible does not condone having more than one wife. God's design for marriage was one man and one woman. Adam and Eve. It wasn't Adam, Eve, and Janet. God said the two would become one flesh. Never in the Scripture does God encourage a man to have more than one wife. Never, not even once. The truth of God's Word isn't changed by what someone may have done that was contrary to its instruction. Truth is truth, and no one can change it.

Who Wins?

Who wins? I mean really, who is going to win today? Today will have some challenges, so will this month or this year—so who will win? It's you against the world. You know, we get afraid sometimes because we don't think we can win, especially when it looks like the world is beating us. Being afraid is a miserable feeling. It's definitely not a happy one. Will you overcome and conquer? Well, I don't have all the answers, but luckily we aren't relying on me for the answer. The answer comes from God and believe me, if He says it, it's true. Here is what God says: "Who is it that overcomes the world? Only he who believes that Jesus is the Son of God" (1 John 5:5). Now you know—you win as long as you believe that Jesus is the Son of God. Notice it didn't say that only the strongest survive or only the smartest, or the tallest guy, or the prettiest girl. Nope, just the one who believes. Why? Because greater is He that is within you than He that is in the world. So stop worrying, because you win.

Ideas

You know that if you ask, the world will give you their ideas. They have ideas about money, dating and marriage. They will tell you about science and how you used to look a lot like an ape. They might give you their philosophy about why it's really cool to drink beer or tell you that you'll have more friends if you smoke. They can even explain how fun it can be to make fun of others or to look at the wrong kind of stuff. The world has an idea about everything, but their plan just isn't working. Colossians 2:8 says, "See to it that no one takes you captive through hollow and deceptive philosophy, which depends on human tradition and the basic principles of this world rather than on Christ." Christ's message is different than the world's. It teaches you to love your enemies, to give, to love your spouse, to have hope, to believe in God the Creator, to take care of your body which is the temple of the Lord, and to have joy in your heart. Christ tells you to keep trying, keep hoping, keep praying, and keep winning. Yes, Christ's message is a different philosophy and here is the good news—it actually works! Tried and proven, it's a message that just won't go away and you can live that message today!

Grace of Forgiveness

Not everyone in your life is going to bail you out when you're in trouble or step up to help you win. So what are you going to do about it? Well, God gives you a clue on what you should do. In 2 Timothy 1, Paul tells Timothy in a letter that while he was in Asia, everyone deserted him. Who would desert Paul? I mean, he's the apostle Paul. Who's leaving that guy? I guess everyone did. They bailed on him when he needed help. So he tells Timothy in chapter 2, verse 1, "You then, my son, be strong in the grace that is in Christ Jesus." What kind of grace is this? It is forgiveness. Paul used his story to develop his student, Timothy. He was saying, "Hey, sometimes people bail on you. So draw on the grace that is in Christ because you are going to need it and it is a lot of grace." Paul was telling Timothy not to get mad at others when they hurt you, but to apply grace. He was saying to forgive others. Don't be surprised—people will let you down. Be prepared to love them anyway. Forgive them and remember that it is God who will never let you down.

What Keeps Its Value

Sometimes the world goes crazy. Proverbs 11:4 says, "Wealth is worthless in the day of wrath, but righteousness delivers from death." This is a funny idea—wealth being worthless. But when the world crashes in around, it is not the money in your bank account, but the character in your heart that matters. Ever notice in your life that events can happen and suddenly money holds no value? Now, this doesn't make wealth bad. It is simply pointing out that righteousness is what is going to count when the storms come. Character, integrity, honesty, faithfulness, love—these things matter. If it is righteousness that delivers us, then it might be good to know how we can be righteous. Remember that because of Christ, you are righteous not by how good you are, but by faith. As it says in Galatians 3:11, "The righteous will live by faith." Faith in whom? In our Savior and Lord Jesus Christ who has announced to us all that He is mighty to save. So, the world may go a little crazy, but the good news is you are righteous and you are joint heirs with Christ. You are delivered not by your own strength or by your money, but by the power of God.

Promises

I was traveling the other day and I told my kids that when I got back, I'd bring them each a little something. It was a promise. You know, God has promises for us too. Many, many promises. My kids were so excited for what I promised them. Are we excited for God's promises? We're excited if we know what they are. In Isaiah 61, it was prophesied that Jesus would come and set us all free. The passage goes on to say that God is going to enter into an everlasting covenant with us, His children. Jesus used His own blood on the cross to cut that covenant with you. It's a covenant that says we are family now. Isaiah 61:9 goes on to say this about us, "All who see them will acknowledge that they are a people the LORD has blessed." That's you. God wants you to stand out. He wants you to be significant. Not only is He saying that He wants to bless you, He is saying He wants to bless you so much that people around will notice. The unbelievers and lost will notice you have favor, wisdom, joy, and peace. It will be apparent that you are different and different in a good way.

A Father You Can Relate To

What's God like? I mean, does He laugh? Psalm 59 says He does. I read this in the Bible the other day and, well, for me, it was a neat way to see another side of God that I hadn't seen before. In Isaiah 47:12 God says, "Keep on then with your magic spells and with your many sorceries... perhaps you will succeed." Is God really telling people to do spells and sorcery, or does He really think such things might succeed? Well, of course not. I think I can relate to the way God is speaking here. He's like, "Go ahead and keep doing the wrong thing, let's see how that works out for you." The more I study the Word, the more I see that God is a Father that I can relate to who sent a Son to live in my shoes. He expresses emotions in His Word. He wants to draw me in and spend time with me, to speak with me, help me, hold me, encourage me, give to me, maybe even tease me when I need a bit of ribbing. I sure love Him.

What Never Changes

The account Genesis gives us describes that initially, God created just one continent, or area of land. Reading in Genesis 1:9 we see, "God said, 'Let the water under the sky be gathered to one place and let dry ground appear.' And It was so." At first, this seemed to contradict the reality that there are seven continents. This meant that science and exploration were suddenly at odds with the Bible. This created quite a stir as exploration continued through the 15th and 16th centuries. But today in school, you will learn it is believed all the continents were connected into just one body of land at one time. Scientists have noticed that all the continents fit together like a puzzle. It took a little while for science to realize that the Bible had it right. Science sometimes seems to disagree with the Bible, but if you just wait, well, every 50 years or so, science changes what it is saying and it always seems to get closer to what God has already said. Don't build your life on something that changes its opinion so often, like science or philosophy. Build your life on the Word and truth, which never changes. Build it on the message that is the same yesterday, today, and forever. Build your life on the message of Christ. It's a rock that cannot be moved.

Learn from Their Mistakes

If you watch the news for more than five minutes, you'll start thinking, "Man, this place is getting pretty messed up." But you know, none of this mess is new. Things were tough when you grew up and they'll be tough for the next generation. The next generation isn't the first to have it hard and it won't be the last. Judges 10:6 says, "Again the Israelites did evil in the eyes of the LORD." Again, yeah, again. It's like they were caught in an endless loop—they did evil, then they hit the bottom (you know everything gets worse when we leave God), then later, the people would return to God and things would get better. When the people would return to God, the blessings would return. God makes things better. Do we want things to get better? Well, the key is to get more of God into our land and more of the people's hearts into God. That may seem like a lot to accomplish, but it isn't. You can make a difference. We don't want to repeat the mistakes of the Israelites of the Bible. We want to be the generation known as the one that turned to the Lord. Share the love of Christ with someone today.

Be Teachable

Proverbs 16:18 says, "Pride goes before destruction." If you want or need more destruction in your life, what you really want is some pride. What is pride? Sometimes people mistake pride for confidence or courage, but this cannot be right since God commanded us to have courage. Certainly Jesus was very confident, as He taught with authority. Pride is something different. Maybe we can best understand pride by thinking of what is the opposite—humility. Norman Vincent Peale once said that humble people don't think less of themselves... they just think of themselves less. Proverbs 11:2 says, "With humility comes wisdom." Humility allows you to learn. You see, when you are filled with pride, you are no longer teachable. This is because you think you already know everything. If you already know everything, then wise counsel will mean nothing. Even the Scripture won't be able to get inside and change you, and as you live thinking you know everything, your pride will lead you right into destruction. Be teachable, listen to others, pay attention to wisdom from grandparents and parents, peers, pastors, and elders. Jesus tells us that even the children can teach us something.

Where to Look for Healing

Did you know that God's original design did not include sickness? The Garden of Eden had a lot of stuff. It had flowers, trees, fruit, streams and animals, but it did not have the flu. The flu and the chicken pox come into play after Adam and Eve sinned and ate the fruit. Now, God isn't the creator of the measles, but He can heal. As Jesus walked with us, He healed all who came to Him. Even before Christ bore our sicknesses on the cross, David was praying to God for healing. "O LORD my God, I called to you for help and you healed me" (Psalm 30:2). Not only was David bold enough to cry out for healing, but he was healed. What's the secret to his healing? David cried out to God. Healing starts with who you look to. If you look to medicine, it might help with the symptoms, but that isn't healing. Jesus heals. How often have we decided that what's afflicting us is just something we have to live with? Instead, start today by asking God for healing. You might say, "I've already tried that." Good—try again, and again, and again. Persevere, be patient, and mostly do not doubt God, but believe He has already provided for your healing.

Rooted

Colossians 2:6-7 says, "So then, just as you received Christ Jesus as Lord, continue to live in Him, rooted and built up in him, strengthened in the faith." Obviously, it was important that you received Christ. Would you say it was one of the most important and best decisions you ever made? I'm sure you would say, "Uh huh, you bet." This scripture says that in the same way you received Christ, you should also live your lives in Him, rooted and built up in Him. What does it mean to be in Him? To be in Him is to be in His body, which is the church. You see, Colossians is a letter to the church. Paul was saying we need to stay connected to the church. Stay in it. It's the body of Christ. So what does it mean to be "rooted"? Psalm 92 describes you as a tree that gets planted. So where should we be planted? In the House of the Lord. Where your roots are is a big deal—nutrients come up through the roots to help the tree grow. Being rooted in a church body is important. Even if you don't perfectly agree with it, go and love anyway. If you don't have a church, get one. Once you have one, stop moving around so much and let your roots grow deep.

Listen

How good of a listener are you? How long can you listen to something? Honestly. Once the teacher starts teaching, how many minutes later is it before you are off in your mind or worse, sleeping? Well, listen up. Joel 1:2 says, "Hear this, you elders; listen, all who live in the land." After saying this, Joel goes on to tell what God is saying. Of course the entire Bible, cover to cover, is God speaking to us, so really in this verse from Joel, it's actually God saying, "Hey, listen up! Don't be distracted or you may miss what I'm trying to tell you." Even thousands of years ago people were distracted, and so are we still today. God was speaking and not everyone was listening. So the question I ask you today is, are you listening? I mean, are you listening to what God is saying? Are we too distracted with life noise, TV and billboards? Are we too distracted to slow down and read our Bibles and go to church? God wants to speak to you today, so listen up!

Plans

What is your plan today? If we want to get something done, we need a plan. Sometimes, like in a family, you have to share your plan so everyone knows what is going on. On Saturdays, my wife has a plan, and I'm a big part of the plan. Especially when there is some stuff to do around the house. But how can I help her be successful in her plans if I don't know the plan? Did you know God has a plan? That's right. He isn't just winging it. He's not flying by the seat of His pants. He has a plan. Sometimes I hear people say, "Well, we don't really know what God's plans are." But Amos 4:13 says, "He who forms the mountains, creates the wind, and reveals his thoughts to man...the LORD God Almighty is his name." If God is revealing His plan to us, maybe we don't know His plan because we aren't looking for His plan. Ask God today about His plan. This world could use some cleaning. There are some chores to do, people to get into the church, people who need help and people who need love. God has a plan for you. And it's a good plan. Now go get it.

Don't Just Stand There

Obadiah 1:11 says, "On the day you stood aloof while strangers carried off his wealth, and foreigners entered his gates and cast lots for Jerusalem, you were like one of them." God is saying, "Hey, I noticed when My people were under attack and others were advancing on My gates, you just stood by and watched." There is a real battle happening every day—a battle where the Kingdom of God is advancing, and the kingdom of darkness is vehemently fighting for territory. Do you ever notice that both good and bad stuff is happening? The question today is, *What is our role?* God does not want us standing around and watching. Maybe we look at the church and say, "Wow, it looks like the church is running out of money. I wonder if they are going to make it?" Stop wondering and get involved. Or maybe your friend is discouraged with life and God or is fighting for her life. Maybe your town needs some new leadership. Do not sit idly by and watch God's territory be attacked. Instead draw up your battle lines and say, "Bring it on!" God is asking you to stand for Him.

On the Way to Hope

Romans 15:4 says, "For everything that was written in the past was written to teach us, so that through endurance and the encouragement of the Scriptures we might have hope." The goal is hope. When God refers to "everything that was written in the past," He is talking about the Bible and is referring to what we now consider the Old Testament. What was the purpose of that writing? This verse says the purpose was to teach us. This means we need to be learning. In this course of this learning, we will need to have endurance. You see, you might read something that says God loves you, but sometimes you don't feel so loved. In this, you might be tempted to give up. But the scripture is asking us to have endurance and keep on going. No quitting! Scripture is encouraging, and who doesn't like encouragement? Through our endurance and the encouragement of Scripture, we will receive hope. Hope is a wonderful thing. Hope has the ability to bring you a smile, even when where you are isn't worth smiling about. Hope says, *Things are getting better.* And, they are. So let's dig in and allow everything that was written in the past to teach us. We've all got some learning to do.

Judgment vs. Acceptance

Romans 14:10 says, "You then, why do you judge your brother...?"
Well it seems not much has changed here. Christians in Paul's day
were judging each other and today we do too. What does it mean to
judge each other? Well, it's when a Christian isn't living up to what
you believe is right. Maybe you judge the way someone is dressed, or
maybe they have a tattoo or piercing, or maybe it's something you saw
them wearing or drinking, or a club you saw them come out of. You
might even say something bad about a church you used to attend. All
of this sometimes causes us to think less of others. The verse goes on
to say, "...or why do you look down on your brother?" Judgment sure
makes us feel better about ourselves doesn't it? We're thinking, "Yeah,
there is someone worse than me." But, God is telling us not to do
this. Later, we're told in Romans 15:7, "Accept one another then, just
as Christ accepted you." How did Christ accept you? Well, while you
were still a sinner, He gave up everything for you. He did not check
your social status or what might be dangling from your ears or that
crazy hair. He accepted you, and we should accept others in the same
way.

Hurt

Have you ever had someone hurt your feelings, or steal from you, or lie about you or to you? When someone has wronged you, what should you do? Well, the natural thing to do is to tell everyone you know what that person did to you, right? It's great juice, and you can always exaggerate what happened to really make that person look bad. You could even make some stuff up to embellish the story. I mean, it's only fair after what they did you to, right? Well, Jesus said in Matthew 18:15, "If your brother sins against you, go and show him his fault, just between the two of you." When you try to settle things just between the two of you, the first thing you might find out is that the whole thing was just a misunderstanding. Maybe you were the one who actually did something wrong and didn't even know it. Maybe by following this instruction, you will avoid having an enemy, and instead you will make a friend. Remember, the goal is to work it out instead of hurting someone back. When you get hurt, it's easy to hurt back. Anyone can do that. But working out your differences, well, that takes work. However, in the end, following God's way to making things right has got to be good.

Bronze Walls

In Jeremiah 1, God called Jeremiah to the ministry and explained to him that he was being made into a fortified city, an iron pillar, a bronze wall. A fortified city is a city that has everything it needs within it to succeed. An iron pillar can withstand a great deal of weight without even feeling pressured. The bronze wall is the first line of defense against the attack of the enemy. But bronze is a most impure metal, symbolizing that we, as humans, are impure. Even leaders, like Jeremiah, are impure because of their humanity. We need to not be surprised and should not be judgmental when those we follow stumble from time to time. Most importantly, never let the stumbles of your leaders steer you away from God. People will be people. This is why we shouldn't put our faith in people; we put our faith in Jesus Christ who is working in our leaders. Submit to your pastors and your spiritual leaders and pray for them. They are honoring the call of God on their lives as best they can with God's help; don't hold them up to a spiritual standard that only Jesus could achieve.

Keeping on Track

Psalm 119:9 asks the question, "How can a young man keep his way pure?" Off the cuff, I would say it's crazy hard to keep a young man's way pure these days. Maybe if you lock him in his room from age 13 to age 19, you might have a chance. I know that would've been helpful for me. But God's Word has a different answer to this question. The Word says, "How can a young man keep his way pure? By living according to your word." The answer is to read God's Word. I was trying to play Bocce ball the other day with my family, but we were doing it all wrong. We weren't playing according to the instructions, because I hadn't read them. Have you read the instructions for life today? How can you keep your life on track? Maybe it would help to read the instructions found in God's Word. We need a little direction every day. Some instruction to keep us going the right direction. Are you struggling to keep your way pure? Get out the Bible every morning and watch everything start turning around for the better.

Feeling Vulnerable

Peter denied Christ three times. Peter was the disciple called to carry Christ's vision, but now, because he was so down on himself for what he had done, Peter went fishing instead. He returned back to what he was doing before he even met Jesus. Jesus appeared on the shore and called out to Peter. When Peter heard Jesus calling to him, it says in John 21:7 that he "wrapped his outer garment around him...and jumped into the water." Now who puts clothes on to go swimming? Why would Peter do this? When people get in the presence of the Lord, they can feel a little vulnerable. It's the same as when Adam and Eve had eaten the fruit, then went and hid and tried to put some clothes on. We feel this way too, sometimes. It's like we're thinking, "How could God possibly use me after what I've done?" But Jesus wasn't concerned with what Peter had done wrong; He was intent on getting him back to work. You don't have to feel exposed in God's presence, or unworthy. Remember that you are clothed in a robe of righteousness! God sees you as blameless and holy because of your faith in Jesus. Get to work. Jesus is not asking you to quit something. He's asking you to start something!

Work

We all want the Garden of Eden life. We want to live in paradise and lay around with nothing on our "to do" list except for … lay around. But in Genesis 2:15, the Bible says, "The LORD God took the man and put him in the Garden of Eden to work it and take care of it." God did not create us to look forward to retirement, but instead to look forward to accomplishment. We are the hands and feet of Christ and there is some work to be done here on earth. The goal isn't to have enough money when you're 35 so you can retire, but to press on toward the prize, the glory of God, by achieving the tasks placed before you. So work hard at everything. Wherever you work, show up early, leave late, take less breaks and give it your all at a greater level of excellence than anyone else all the time. Study your job and those around and above you so that you will be ready for promotion when positions open. Make yourself irreplaceable. This is the kind of example a Christian should be, sending a message to the world that Christians tear it up on the job. You should always be doing your best as though you are working for the Lord, for that is where your reward is going to come from anyway.

The Right Remedy

Know your medicine in life! If you have a headache, you don't go to the foot doctor. If you have a problem with anger, you wouldn't ask the person who cuts your hair to help. God outlines in His Word remedies for everything we go through. If we are experiencing trials in our life, the remedy is perseverance, not quitting. If the problem is a sin we keep doing, the remedy is God's grace through His Son, Jesus Christ. And when our problem is feelings of condemnation, a good dose of God's mercy allows us to continue to serve Him. If you are experiencing an actual physical disease or an injury, the remedy God provides throughout His Word is healing. He sent His Word and healed our disease. By the stripes of Jesus, the beatings He took during His crucifixion, we are healed. So make sure that whatever you are going through in your life, you have the right remedy.

For the Ladies

Have you heard the saying, "It's a man's world"? Sometimes women don't feel like the world values them and the wisdom God has given them. Society, for many years, has presented women as being less than men. But there's good news ladies. God doesn't feel that way. In Judges 4, God had a woman running things. The Bible says that Deborah, a prophetess, was leading Israel. One day, the word of the Lord came to her that all of Israel was to be delivered from the Caananites. God spoke through her to the commander of Israel's army, and she instructed him exactly how Israel was to defeat the Caananites. Deborah was telling him what to do according to God's will. Ladies—God will speak through you. Paul writes that in Christ, there is neither male nor female, meaning that all are equal in Christ. Now if we could just get the rest of the world to think that way. Ladies, God has a word for you, He has a plan for your life, and He needs you to help Him. The world should thank God daily for you.

Right Size Armor

When David was going to take on the giant Goliath, they had him try on King Saul's armor and sword. But, it wasn't right. Nothing fit. David couldn't use someone else's armor and sword for his battle. He needed to find the weapon that would suit him for his situation. He used a sling and some rocks and Goliath took one in the head. You have giants to fight in your life. And quite often, someone who means well will attempt to tell you how they would handle the situation. They will try to give you their armor and sword. But it probably won't fit quite right. You need to do like David. Go to the Word and let God arm you with the armor of the Lord and the sword of the Spirit. God has the perfect solution to your problem. When you trust God and come out victorious, your story will serve as an example of why it is best to trust God, instead of trusting in the advice of man. You will often find wisdom in counsel—David did try on Saul's armor—but if you find it doesn't fit your situation, don't give up. Go to the Bible. God is our Rock. He can defeat your giant.

A Lesson in Wishing from Solomon

Let's say you found a genie lamp and you get one wish. What do you wish for? (You cannot wish for more wishes!) One common answer is money. But when God told King Solomon that He would give him whatever he asked, Solomon asked for wisdom, specifically, discernment so that he would be able to judge between the people that he was in charge of. He wanted something to help him with his God-given purpose. We could learn from this. You can pray for the tools and abilities to help you be great at the things God gives you to do. Too often we are seeking things, but that doesn't seem to be what Solomon was seeking. For instance, we might ask God for a better job. Instead, we could ask Him to make us a better employee at our current job. We ask God for a new house, a new car, or we pray fervently for a big LCD TV. But not Solomon. The thing is, even though King Solomon didn't ask for wealth, he ended up richer than anyone living in his time. It's not that money was the key to happiness, but for Solomon, prosperity was a result of doing what God had asked him to do. Sounds a lot like seeking first God's kingdom, and then all the other things are added.

When Friends Mess Up

In Luke 22, Peter told Jesus, "Lord I am ready to go with you to prison and to death." But Jesus answered, "I tell you, Peter, before the rooster crows today, you will deny three times that you know me." Sure enough, Jesus was put on trial and then crucified and where was Peter? Peter didn't even go to see his Lord on the cross. When people said, "Hey, didn't you work with Jesus?" Peter denied even knowing Him. This was one of Jesus' closest friends. Listen, if Jesus' friends got scared, denied Him, and even betrayed Him as Judas did, then you can know your friends will do the same to you. Even close friends are going to mess up sometimes. Remember, your friends are human and just like you, they may blow it. Remember how Jesus handled the situation with Peter. He forgave Peter and restored their friendship. In the same way, give your friends grace, forgive them. Let them know that they hurt you, but love them enough to do whatever it takes to restore the friendship.

Seeing the Face of Jesus

Matthew, Mark, Luke and John all tell the story of Christ. The New Testament tells Christ's story four times. Why? Well, probably for a lot of reasons, but one reason is that each book presents a different face of Christ. Ezekiel 1:10 prophesied about this 500 years before Jesus was born. Ezekiel had a vision of four living creatures, "Their faces looked like this: Each of the four had the face of a man, and on the right side each had the face of a lion, and on the left the face of an ox, and each also had the face of an eagle." The living creature represents the living Word of God. The face of the man represents the humanity of Jesus, who became a man and is represented in the book of Luke. The face of the lion represents the king, Jesus the King of kings, which is the story as told by Matthew. The face of the ox represents Jesus the servant, as portrayed in the book of Mark. Finallhy, the eagle represents diety, which is Jesus Christ, the Son of God. As John says in Chapter 1, the Word was with God and the Word was God. Jesus—He is man, king, servant, and God. The four gospels were all promised to us by God through the prophet Ezekiel. Do you want to see Jesus' face? You can! Just read His stories.

It's Up to You

Raise your hand if you still live with Mom and/or Dad. Whether you still live with your parents or not, I've got something for you to consider. Today, I want you to begin to own your relationships with your parents and brothers and sisters. What do I mean? Well, let's think about this. If you still live at home, how many years will it be until you think you will be moving out? How do you want to remember those years? Do you want to remember them as fun or annoying? Do you want to remember them for the yelling matches with your parents, or for the laughter and fun? Of course you want to remember them as happy years. So what can you do to help make great memories? You see, it's your family too, whether it's good or bad doesn't have to be all up to Mom and Dad. You can choose to make things better. What if they are really stressed at work and doing their best, and maybe the bills are stacking up, what can you do? You could pick up around the house or ask Mom if there is anything she needs help with. You could choose to ditch your friends and ask your parents to a movie and tell them you are paying. You could hug them when they don't ask for it, thank them when you don't feel like it, and change your behavior when they ask. How much better will these last few years be? It's kind of up to you, isn't it?

Flourish

Psalm 92:12-13 says, "The righteous...planted in the house of the LORD, they will flourish in the courts of our God." Now I don't know about you, but I want to flourish in my life. I am righteous, not because I'm perfect, but because of my faith in Jesus Christ, so I'm qualified to flourish. But there is one other key to flourishing. I must be planted in the house of the Lord. The house of the Lord is church. If this verse says we should be planted there, then church isn't just somewhere you go; it is a place you are planted. Picture yourself as a tree. You have roots. Where are your roots? God wants them in your church. The church has water—the Word of God—flowing from it so your roots can get good and wet to keep you growing and flourishing. You might say that you don't like church, but the Bible is telling us to be planted in church. Ephesians chapters 1 and 2 tell us that the church is the body of Christ and the dwelling place of the Lord. We know that Christ lives in you as well, so imagine how awesome it would be to bring God, who is in you, to your church. Find a place to serve, honor the Lord with your wealth, listen to the Word of God preached, and help the congregation reach the community and the world for the Lord. Get your roots in there good and deep. Keep in mind, it is not easy for a tree to just uproot itself and walk somewhere else. To be rooted means to be committed. Get committed, get rooted in church, and get to flourishing.

Work Hard

Society, and even friends, will tell you that you should work just hard enough to not get fired. After all, you need your lunch break and two or three more 15-minute breaks. Forty hours a week is plenty. Any more than that and you need overtime pay. When's my day off, anyway? Jesus told a parable in Matthew 20:6. In it He said, "About the eleventh hour he went out and found still others standing around. He asked them, 'Why have you been standing here all day long doing nothing?'" You see, God wants us working. He wants us producing. In fact, Jesus points out in John 15:2 that if you aren't producing, you will be cut off from the tree. Paul taught that if you don't work, you don't eat (2 Thessalonians 3:10). There was a fig tree that Jesus cursed solely because it looked like it was producing fruit but wasn't (Matthew 21:18-19). God, by His own example, set up a system of six days of work and one day of rest each week. Hard work is just being faithful. When you start really working hard, skipping breaks, showing up early for work and working late to get the job done, you are honoring God. He will reward you. Don't work for a 'thank you' or even for a raise. Work hard because God asks you to. Then, it doesn't matter what others are doing or saying, you know in your heart why you do what you do. Do more than you are asked, faster and better than anyone else. Then you are setting yourself up for great success.

Different

Jesus said in Matthew 16:25, "For whoever wants to save his life will lose it, but whoever loses his life for me will find it." Huh? If I want life, I have to lose it? Well now, this is a different way of thinking. Following Christ and being a Christian is a different way of living. Nearly every idea you will find on television, in the movies, in the locker room or in society in general will be about how to find happiness, yet these ideas will all be opposite of what God teaches us. The world is about doing what you want or doing what feels good. But being a Christian means living a very different way of life and having a very different way of thinking than most of the world. So when your decisions don't fit in with everyone else's, that's good. Being a Christian means being different. This difference will bring you a good life. You will have a blessed life, with a lot less drama than everyone else. You will have happiness. Jesus is promising this. Those who are all about their own lives are going to lose. Jesus said it would be so. But when we decide to put others and God above our own needs, when we remind our own body that it is not in charge of us, and instead we choose things like trustworthiness, faithfulness, honesty, integrity, and character, then we will truly find life. Choose to not be led by your desires, but be led by God. God will meet your desires far more than the world ever could. Lose your life and then you find it. Enjoy being different.

Seeds

One time, I was carving a pumpkin, cutting off the top and scooping out the seeds. It's kind of a nasty job actually, and really goopy. I was thinking as I worked, *Man, that's a lot of seeds.* In one pumpkin, I counted 51 seeds. In farmer language, that's a 50-fold return. One pumpkin had 51 seeds. As I looked through the seeds, I was surprised to see that in amongst the pumpkin seeds was an apple seed and a few almonds. Now, how did a pumpkin produce an apple seed and almonds? OK, that's actually not what I saw. There were actually only pumpkin seeds. But you knew that would be the case, didn't you? No one since the creation of the world has found corn seeds in a watermelon. Whatever seed you plant, it grows that type of crop and produces more of that seed. This is the principle of reaping what you sow. Now, think about your own life—what does your fruit currently look like? Take inventory of your life fruit. If you want different fruit than what you are currently producing, you will have to plant different seeds in your future. This is a principle of God. If your brother is always mad at you, think about what you sowed in him. If no one is helping you, maybe you haven't been very helpful. Do you need a miracle in your life? Many of the prayers for miracles that were offered up, like Hannah praying for a baby or King David praying for the healing of the land, were accompanied by an offering. These people sowed a seed into the kingdom of God with their prayers. What you are sowing today will produce fruit in your future. Sow wisely.

NOVEMBER 8

Smart People

Did you know there are some people who don't believe in God? Really, it's true. You can often hear people trying to convince others that God does not exist and that all this glorious creation, the vastness of the universe, the rain on our skin, our ability to see, hear, taste, smell, touch is all an accident. But do you know that the most highly esteemed scientists in history and today have come to the inescapable conclusion that all of this could only have come from God? Who are these really smart scientists you ask? These include people like astrophysicist Bernard Haisch, who started in his field as an athiest but found the undeniable proof of God's existence in his study of the universe. There's quantum theory founder Max Planck, or Galileo, or Sir Isaac Newton, or Robert Boyle, or Michael Faraday, or Gregor Mendel, the author of modern genetics. Or today's top microbiologist, Michael Behe, who was an athiest, but is now born again. Or consier the man who is the most well known genius of all time, Albert Einstein. Yeah, he believed in God too. All this to show that the smart people, they believe in God.

Dwelling

Where do you dwell? I mean, where is your dwelling? You'd probably answer in your house or apartment. Okay, so where does God dwell? He dwells in His house. First Timothy 3:15 says that God's household is the church, which is us. The church is a group of believers who come together to hear the Word of God and worship Him. Psalm 90:1 says, "Lord, you have been our dwelling place." So if we put all this together, we find out that God wants us to dwell where He dwells. Let's be sure we understand—God is dwelling where believers dwell and He wants us to dwell where He dwells, which again is exactly where we are when we come together as believers. Are you confused yet? Well, just grab hold of this, because it's the coolest part—God wants to be and is, with you. He desires to have you with Him, which you are. Even more awesome, He has promised to never leave you or forsake you. Sometimes you might feel like God is not around, but His Word is true which means He is with you. What you may be craving is to get back into church. Make your church more than a place you visit. Make it your church home.

Call Your Ally

Have you ever tried to do something God called you to do, but it seemed like an uphill battle that you were losing. In I Thessalonians 2, Paul states that he wanted to go see the Thessalonians. He explains, however, in verse 18, "For we wanted to come to you – certainly I, Paul, did again and again—but Satan stopped us." Paul knew who was trying to stop him, and that was Satan. Paul put the blame where the blame was due. Now, Satan has been defeated by Christ, but still sometimes the enemy tries to stop us from doing something God has called us to. Hey, if Paul was stopped sometimes, then don't get discouraged when you hit a road block. Paul didn't give up or act defeated but instead, in chapter 3 and verse 11, Paul prayed, "Now may our God and Father himself and our Lord Jesus clear the way for us to come to you." Follow Paul's example and if there is any fighting to do with Satan, get God involved. Get some prayer going! Don't fight by yourself, but ask God for help. And like Paul, make sure you know who to blame when things are going wrong. So what happened to Paul? Well, about three years later, Paul did return to the Thessalonians. God wins again! And when God wins, you win.

When You've Been Wronged

Have you ever been treated unfairly, wronged, abused, or violated? So what do you do with all that? Did you get mad, feel hurt, or allow the bad images to replay in your mind? You know, Jesus went through tough times. He was horribly wronged, prosecuted and punished unjustly. He was mocked, beaten, bruised, publicly humiliated, and killed. And yet we see in Luke 23:34 that Jesus cried, "Father, forgive them, for they do not know what they are doing." Interesting. Jesus was saying that the people crucifying Him did not know they were doing wrong. Jesus asked God to forgive them. When we're hurt, sometimes at first we might want God to go get the ones who have hurt us, not forgive them. We want to say something mean to the ones who hurt us or write a letter or email, but that isn't the example Jesus set. So, how should we react? Jesus shows us that the right reaction is love. It's a better reaction because our mean words don't make anything better. They usually make things worse. Instead, ask God for the strength to forgive and ask that He forgive them too. Now, this is the right answer.

Don't Fight—We're on the Same Team

Have you ever asked someone to do something and then when they didn't do it, you got mad at them? "I thought I told you to take out the trash!" Sometimes, good Christians treat God in this manner. You may have prayed for something important, and it didn't happen fast enough, and so you found yourself arguing with God. But Isaiah 45:9 says "Woe to him who quarrels with his Maker." Woe. That's not good—woe is like distress or bitter regret. No one wants any of that. You see when Jesus died, He provided all victory for you as He breathed His final words, "It is finished." With that, He defeated the powers of darkness, sickness, death, sin, and He nailed to the cross lust, deceit, and shame. Further, He gave you His Word, poured out His love, and placed the same Spirit that raised Christ from the dead within you. You have the mind of Christ and the armor of the Lord and God himself has promised to be a shield around you and a mighty fortress. When we fight with God, we are acting as though He is the enemy, but to defeat the real enemy we need God's mighty hand on our team. So no more fighting with God. He's on your team!

Love Matters

Jesus said in Matthew 5 that if you are giving to God then suddenly remember your brother is upset with you, you need to leave your gift, go be reconciled to your brother, then come back and give. In Malachi 2:13-14, we see God was not pleased with the gifts of the people and the reason He stated was this "The Lord is acting as the witness between you and the wife of your youth, because you have broken faith with her." In both of these cases, gifts to God were affected by relationships—one with a brother or sister in the Lord, the other with a spouse. What is God saying here? Well, He's telling us how important it is that we get along with each other. He's saying that we show Him we love Him when we love others. First John 4:20 says, "Anyone who does not love his brother, whom he has seen, cannot love God, whom he has not seen." God just wants us all to get along. If you got married, then love your spouse and do it well. Love your neighbor, love your brother, and in this way, you are loving God and your gifts to Him are like that of Abel who loved and not like that of Cain, who did not love.

Be Careful What You Say

In Job 1:11 Satan told God, "Stretch out your hand and strike everything he (Job) has, and he will surely curse you to your face." Now God didn't stretch out His hand and do any striking (in case you are wondering). He gave Satan permission to do what Satan does, and that is to destroy things. Now, don't go into fear that Job's story is going to happen to you. Remember that Jesus died on the cross and changed everything. Job didn't have a Redeemer like we do! All the stories you read in the Old Testament must be washed through the cross. Things have certainly changed. You are highly favored, blessed and well protected as the righteous of the Lord. But notice what Satan's goal was. His goal was to change how Job spoke about God. His goal was to get Job to curse God. What we speak is so very important. It is with words that God created the heavens and earth, and when Zechariah spoke doubt out loud about the coming of John the Baptist, the angel closed his mouth and he could not speak until the baby was born. So what are you saying? How do you describe God? Are you describing your mess or are you speaking what God says? Both God and Satan are interested in what you say—choose your words wisely.

Invest in Your Mind

How important is your education? God has given you a mind, but it's up to you to use it and to invest in it. In the parable of talents, Jesus tells of three people each given different amounts of money. The two who invested the money were rewarded, but the one who did nothing with what he was given (the one who buried it) got in trouble. God has given us a mind and we need to invest in it and take care of it. Moses was chosen to lead the Israelites out of Egypt. Moses, the only Israelite not raised as a slave in Egypt, as he was raised by the Pharaoh's daughter in the palace, was probably highly educated. The apostle Paul was highly educated, having spent his life studying under the great Hebrew philosopher, Gamaliel (Acts 22:3). If Paul had not known how to read and write both the languages Greek and Hebrew, he would not have been able to write so much of the New Testament. But his learning put him in position to proclaim Jesus Christ's righteousness to a people yet unborn. So whatever educational course you decide to follow, remember that your brain is a valuable tool. Don't ignore a tool God has given you.

Overflowing

In 2 Kings 4, we see the story of a woman whose husband dies and leaves her with a lot of debt. Unlike today when the worst that might happen is a person might lose their house or car, this woman was about to lose her two sons to slavery in order to pay off her debt. Wow, you thought your creditors were rough! She asked the prophet Elijah for help and he asked her, "What do you have?" (v. 2). Well, the woman had a little oil. Elijah told her to gather as many jars as she could; to ask all her neighbors for extra jars. She did this. Then Elijah told her to pour the oil she had into each jar that she collected. By a miracle of God, the oil kept flowing until every jar was filled. The woman sold the oil and paid off her debt. You may find in your life you sometimes have need. Ask God to help. God wants to fill your jars with whatever you need and He is looking for you to use whatever you have to the best of your ability. How many jars can you believe God to fill? It seems to me that in this story, God would have filled as many jars as the woman could've gotten her hands on. God wants to fill you up to overflowing. What do you need? Peace? Joy? Health? Wealth? Well, go get some jars and start pouring.

Don't Walk Away

In John 6, Jesus was teaching His followers when a group of them disagreed with Jesus. Here's a rule of thumb: Never disagree with the Son of God. Sadly, these guys turned away and no longer followed Jesus. In hindsight, I wonder if these disciples ever realized how much they really missed the boat. They missed what Jesus was really saying. They walked away from the Messiah. How were so many duped into walking away? This same kind of thing happens in churches across this nation. Someone disagrees with the pastor and before you know it, a group of people leave the church. If this happened to Jesus, it can happen to your pastor. Don't get sucked into this mess. Stay far away from these kinds of people. Their words may seem right, and you may be tempted to follow the exodus, but you should stay true to the body of Christ you are planted in. You need to have your pastor's back. Don't let someone disrespect your pastor. The devil wants to uproot you out of the church. He wants you to become disconnected and discouraged. Don't let him win.

Thankful Always

When I take my kids to get ice cream, inevitably, when it's all gone, my youngest will start crying, "I want more." I understand why he's crying because I want more too. But then a part of me thinks, *Hey, just be thankful for what you got.* Sounds like something my dad would've said. God will send ice cream moments into your life, but not all moments are ice cream moments. Being thankful to God shouldn't be dependent on everything being golden today. You should be thankful because you recognize that God loves you and that He desires for you to have joy and He wants to give you some ice cream in life. Unlike the ice cream that's all sugary and fattening, God's promises are wonderful for you. In 1 Chronicles 23:30, the priests were required to "stand every morning to thank and praise the LORD. They were to do the same in the evening." This wasn't an optional thank you, and it didn't matter whether the priests were grumpy that day (or had run out of ice cream). I think we can learn from this. We are called a royal priesthood—let's get thankful every morning and every night!

Another Way to Say Thanks

I really like my wife. I mean, I really love her, and sometimes I want to thank her for tolerating me. But how can I say thank you besides just saying the words? There are actually many ways we can thank others. Psalm 30:4 says, "Sing to the LORD, you saints of His; praise his holy name." This verse tells us to offer God a *song* of thanksgiving. So maybe one way I can be thankful is to sing. Now I don't know that my wife would want to hear me singing a song to her, but you know who does? God. Every week at church, songs are sung to thank God. Notice, though, in this scripture, singing a song of thanks isn't a suggestion, but it really is a command. Now maybe not all of us are great singers, but no matter how bad we might sound, our hearts can have a glorious song for the Lord. Our heart songs can say, "Thanks for loving me, thanks for the breath, thanks for Your Son, thanks for Rice Krispie treats, and of course, thanks be to Your holy name." Praise God! Amen!

Power

Do you ever yell at someone because they make you SO MAD? How powerful is your yelling? Psalm 29:9 says, "The voice of the Lord twists the oaks and strips the forests bare." Now, I couldn't twist an oak with my hands, but God can do it with just His voice. He can take out a forest with just a word. God's words are powerful. Wow, don't you just wish you had access to that kind of power! I don't know if you have some oaks in your world that could use some twisting—maybe there's a problem that has taken root in your Garden of Eden—but if you do, it would be great to have access to this kind of oak-twisting power. But where can we access God's spoken word? Hmmm… ever thought of trying the Bible? You see, you do have access to that power. God has a bunch of words He has already spoken over your life. He has instructed you in depth and has given you the tools to succeed. He is ready to do great things in your life. Now, crack open that Bible and check out the power that is there for use in your life.

What the Blessing Brings

Proverbs 10:22 says, "The blessing of the LORD brings wealth, and he adds no trouble to it." The blessing brings wealth, but without trouble. Well, has God given you the blessing? Let me answer—yes He has. Galatians 3:14 says that Christ redeemed us so that the blessing of Abraham would be given to us. Now, this blessing brings wealth but this wealth has no trouble added to it. Can wealth bring trouble? Yes it can. Jesus warned us that chasing money or making money our master would mess us up. But this is a different situation. Notice the verse from Proverbs says it is the blessing that brings the wealth. It isn't you bringing it; it's God. You aren't your source—God is your source. Why would the blessing bring you wealth? In 2 Corinthians 9:11 Paul writes, "You will be made rich in every way so that you can be generous on every occasion." You see, when all your bills are paid and you have some joy, some peace, some love, and some extra dough in your pocket, then you can be generous in meeting the needs of this world.

Thanksgiving

On Thanksgiving every year, a lot of people make a journey from house to house, eating several turkeys, casseroles, and some crazy stuffing where you spend the majority of your time trying to identify exactly what that green and yellow stuff is that's mixed in there. But what is Thanksgiving really about? The Bible contains the word *thank* 144 times. So what are you thankful for and can you express it? Can you communicate to all the people around you and to your God what you are appreciative for this year? David wrote in Psalm 100:4, "Enter his gates with thanksgiving and his courts with praise; give thanks to him and praise his name." We enter the gates of God by being thankful in our heart. We live in a world that is all about what we don't have and what we need to have. Instead, we need to focus on what we do have. And if you can't think of something to be thankful for, how about the breath you just took? You're still breathing, right? The greatest gift we have is the gift of life. We can thank Jesus for giving us the breath of life and for giving up His life that we could have eternal life with Him.

Check Your Expectations

Have you ever said, "Ughhhh, I'm just dreading tomorrow. I don't like it when I have to… (fill in the blank)." You know, how we approach a day will determine our happiness and success in that day. When we approach a day with *UGGGH*, we are starting out expecting to barely get by and to be miserable. Guess what? You might just get what you expect. If you have to do something, you might as well enjoy it. That way you are happy and much more likely to succeed. If you are good at the things you enjoy, then learn to enjoy the things you aren't good at. In Phillipians 3:1 Paul says, "Finally, my brothers, rejoice in the Lord!" So take a deep breath. Today is great and tomorrow is going to be great. Love your family, your friends, your church, love your life and most of all, thank God for something. Rejoice! What will today bring? Well, how about success and happiness? That's what I'm expecting.

How to Be Successful in Prayer

I heard a song on the radio the other day that has a line where the singer says, "Just praying to a God that I don't believe in." That's a weird statement. Why pray if you don't believe? I need to send that dude a letter and tell him about Jesus. You know, many who don't believe in God have nowhere to turn when they need a miracle. When you need a prayer answered, what you believe matters. Here's what I mean. Jesus said in Mark 11:24, "Whatever you ask for in prayer, believe that you have received it, and it will be yours." There are many important keys to effective prayer and here is one—you need to believe. When Peter tried walking on the water and then began to sink, Jesus said he started sinking because of his lack of faith. Many times when Jesus healed, He would tell the person that it was their faith that had healed them. Faith is what you believe. What are you praying for? Believe that you have received it. If Jesus taught us how to pray more effectively, it means He wants you to be successful in your praying.

Take Up My Case

I was in front of a judge once for a speeding ticket. Uhh, yeah, I sped. Now I know you never speed, but I did. So there I was, I paid my fine and off I went. My experience got me to thinking, when it comes to doing right and wrong, the judge holds us accountable, to be, well, just. Now, who is the ultimate judge? This would be God, right? So if I'm in front of God to be judged, it would be a lot different than standing in front of the traffic court judge. I mean, the only thing the traffic court judge knew about me was that I had been speeding. But God knows a lot more than that. Come to think of it, I might need a lawyer... I found some good news in Lamentations 3:58: "O Lord, you took up my case; you redeemed my life." So if God is the judge, who has redeemed your life? Jesus has! And He has taken up your case. Now if there was ever anyone you would want on your side, taking up your case, it's Jesus. He is presenting your defense. Now that's good news!

To be Seen or Not to be Seen

In Matthew 5:16 Jesus says, "Let your light shine before men, that they may see your good deeds and praise your Father in heaven." Now, in the same Sermon on the Mount, Jesus says, "Be careful not to do your 'acts of righteousness' before men, to be seen by them" (Matthew 6:1). So which is it? Well of course, it's both. Jesus' message is not a shallow one, but it is rich in depth and wisdom. For this reason, we want to get into the Bible and dig deep. The difference between the situations Jesus described was the intent of the heart. Jesus' message wasn't about the detailed rules of everything you need to do, instead it dealt with issues concerning the inside of you, and who He wants you to be. Jesus was saying what is important is your heart intentions, not just your actions. Obviously, we want to be a good example. But we don't do good stuff just so people will think we are super cool. We should do right because it is the right thing to do. With this mindset, you do the right thing whether people are looking or not. It's just part of who you are.

Getting It Right

Imagine I'm riding in the car with you, in the seat right next to you, and I tell you, "Man, you stink." So you go home and shower and put some deodorant on, but maybe I wasn't talking about your smell. Maybe I meant your driving stinks. It's really easy to misunderstand people isn't it? This is going to happen, but you know what we don't want to misunderstand? We don't want to misunderstand the Word of God. For this reason, Jesus sent us a Teacher. He says in John 14:25 "The Counselor, the Holy Spirit, whom the Father will send in my name, will teach you all things and will remind you of everything I have said to you." God does not want to be misunderstood. Ask God to help you understand His Word. He has sent you His Spirit to help you do just that. Also, you must be hearing and reading the word of God daily. Only when you hear the Word can the Holy Spirit remind you of everything you've heard. Get more Bible in you so the Holy Spirit has something to remind you of.

Better than You Might Think

Have you ever quit something because you felt like you weren't any good at it? In Acts 7:22, Stephen was describing Moses to the people and he said this, "Moses was educated in all the wisdom of the Egyptians and was powerful in speech and action." Moses grew up in the Egyptian Palace, so he was quite used to talking to Egyptian royalty. Now think back to the Moses and the burning bush story found in Exodus 3. Moses told God he couldn't speak well enough to talk to Pharaoh. But Stephen described Moses as powerful in speech. Interesting. Apparently Moses was powerful in speech, he just didn't know it. In fact, he was the perfect man for the job, the perfect choice to go and talk to Pharaoh. God knew it, but Moses didn't know it. God is choosing you to do something that you may not think you can do. You might be thinking, "Oh, I'm not good enough at this or that." What's funny is, if God says you are, then you are. He made you. You can do all things through Christ who strengthens you (Philippians 4:13). You are amazing, wonderful, the righteousness of God.

Pray Also for Me

Paul was a powerful man of the Lord. Yet Paul wrote in Ephesians 6:19, "Pray also for me, that whenever I open my mouth words may be given me so that I will fearlessly make known the mystery of the gospel." Paul asked for prayer. Paul, the great apostle who planted and led churches across the land, whose hand wrote some of God's words for us to read 2,000 years later—Paul who saw miracles and the impossible, who saw angels, who met Jesus on the road to Damascus—even that guy knew when he needed others to pray for him. There are two things I get from this. First, never be afraid to ask others to pray with you. There is power in prayer, it is an advantage we have over this world. We can include God in our world….we can pray. If Paul could ask for prayer, then so can you. Second, our leaders need prayer sometimes. They give and give and give, but who stops to pray for them? Even Jesus, on the night He was betrayed, asked His disciples to pray for Him. Do you need prayer? How about the guy next to you at work, does he need prayer? We all do.

Exalt God

Johsua 3:7 says, "The LORD said to Joshua, 'Today I will begin to exalt you in the eyes of all Israel, so they may know that I am with you as I was with Moses.'" We exalt God, but here it says God was going to exalt Joshua. Why? Well, it was so the people would know that God was with him. Now let me ask this… Is God with you? If you've chosen Christ to be your Lord and savior, then God has promised to never leave you nor forsake you, which means He is with you now. God shows that you are His as He raises you up. One thing you should know is that Joshua did not desire to exalt himself. King David's sons tried to exalt themselves and it didn't work. But if God is with you and your heart is set on service to others and to God, then don't be surprised when God wants people to see that He is with you. God wants people to know that you are His, and that He is yours. He is raising His children up as an example to the whole world. Sometimes when people get raised up they might say, "Oh no God, I'm not worthy," but you are worthy. Jesus made sure of that!

The Word Became Flesh

John 1:1 says, "In the beginning was the Word, and the Word was with God, and the Word was God." The passage continues and in verse 14 we see, "The Word became flesh and made his dwelling among us." Did you hear that? The Word became flesh. That Word is Jesus Christ. He is the Word of God. Now when Jesus spoke words, stuff would happen. He would tell the crippled hand to stretch out, and *boom*, it would. He told dead Lazarus to "Come forth," and he did. God's words have the power to bring life, to move mountains, to heal. They hold supernatural power, power for a new beginning. God may have been thinking about creating the universe, but nothing happened until He SPOKE. Everything came into action when He simply said, "Let there be…." Do you need change in your world? How about a new start? God gave you His Word, the Word of God, the Bible. You see, we can speak God's words into our world. We can pray for the sick and they will recover. We can cast some mountains into the sea. Are you ready for a brand new beginning? Get out that Bible and speak God's words into your world.

Be It Unto Me

So I heard Santa Claus is coming to town. If you you really think about it, though, a man sneaking down your chimney in the middle of the night could be a bit creepy. The truth is, Jesus already came to town 2000 years ago, and He brought us the gift of life. He's not eating my cookies or sneaking around my house; He leaves the gift He brings in my heart. The angel of the Lord visited Mary and said, "You will be with child and give birth to a son, and you are to give him the name Jesus" (Luke 1:31). Well this was BIG. So what did Mary say? Did she say, "No way, not me… I'm not good enough, I'm not worthy!" No, in Luke1:38 she says, "May it be to me as you have said." You see, Mary had the right answer, she believed.Like Mary, God desires to birth His word in your heart, too. When we hear His words, His plans to bless us and keep us safe, His promises of a long life and happiness, let's say what Mary said. Don't say, "Oh, that kind of thing never works out for me." Instead let's say, "Be it unto me as you have said."

Not a Surprise

Have you ever wondered why the gifts under the tree are wrapped? Of course it's because that way you don't know what is in them. It's a surprise. But the greatest gift of all was Jesus, and His coming was not a surprise. God told us ahead of time that He was coming. He said in Isaiah 7:14, "Therefore the Lord himself will give you a sign: The virgin will be with child and will give birth to a son, and will call him Immanuel." About 800 years later, sure enough, it happened just like God said it would. You can count over 400 prophecies spanning 4,000 years, of God alerting the world that His biggest gift was coming. This gift wasn't wrapped in glitter and bows, but came to us wrapped in cloth and laying in a manger. Our gift, Jesus, then died during the Passover feast, a feast created to memorialize the Hebrews leaving slavery. Jesus was our Passover Lamb, whose blood was shed to bring us life and bring us out of slavery to this world. Psalm 22 prophesied of the cross and mentions that the Christ's hands and feet would be pierced and His clothes divided up by casting lots. God didn't hide His gift from us. Let's not hide that gift either. Tell someone about Jesus and what He has done for you.

Chestnuts and Jack Frost

I have something to admit. I have never had chestnuts roasting on an open fire, and Jack Frost has never nipped at my nose. I live in the city, where open fires in the street are "frowned upon." And I've been quite successful at keeping Jack away from my big nose to this point. So these things don't remind me of Christmas. To me, Christmas is a reminder of stuff like Isaiah 9:6, which says, "For to us a child is born, to us a son is given, and the government will be on his shoulders. And he will be called Wonderful Counselor, Mighty God, Everlasting Father, Prince of Peace." This is a reminder that God is bringing good gifts to us, good things into our life. He has given up a lot to make your life better. Now, there is a real devil and a messed up world, both of which might try to make your life worse. But God is on your side, and He has given all to you. Remember, to us a child is born—a Wonderful Counselor, Mighty God, and Everlasting Father. This was done that we might receive life, joy, and peace.

Highway Through the Desert

Malachi 3:1 says, "See, I will send my messenger, who will prepare the way before me." In Isaiah 40:3 it says, "In the desert prepare the way for the Lord; make straight in the wilderness a highway for our God." This messenger who is mentioned in both passages is John the Baptist, who prepared the highway through the wilderness for Jesus. Why would he prepare a *highway*? Well, God **wanted** a highway through the wilderness. You see, God never intended for the Israelites to be stuck in the wilderness for so long. Sure, we all may go through the wilderness to get to God's Promised Land, but we aren't supposed to die in the wilderness. Our path through the wilderness should be a highway. Jesus was in the wilderness for 40 days, where He fasted and was tempted. How many of us get stuck in the wilderness? We might even think, "Well, this is my lot in life." Get on the highway! John the Baptist paved the road, then Jesus drove the road, and you are supposed to follow Him. He is like your own police escort into the things of God. God is calling us out of slavery, out of the wilderness, and into His Promised Land. So put the top down, get on the freeway, and step on the gas.

Better News

The angels were busy as Christ was getting ready to be born. Some angels went to some shepherds to announce Christ's arrival on the scene. It says Luke 2:10, "But the angel said to them, 'Do not be afraid. I bring you good news of great joy that will be for all the people.'" You know, our normal reaction to change is fear. If I was used to seeing fields and sheep, and suddenly a bright light shines out there and an angel starts talking, well, I'd be afraid. God brings change into our lives, but He wants us to not be afraid. I know that sometimes the news you get can be bad news, but God's news is good news. He has good news for you today. God's news is described as bringing great joy, not just a little joy. And this news is for all of us. All people. Anyone, no matter where they are, who they are, or what they have done, can receive Christ and have full access to the covenant God has made with us. So fear not, there's good news that should bring great joy for all men. We have a good God.

Whatcha Giving?

So, what do you want for Christmas? That's the question lots of people ask, isn't it? And there is nothing wrong with that. But I have a different question. What are you getting your mom for Christmas? Or your dad, brother or sister, or whoever happens to be in your world taking care of you? This is your *family*. What are you giving? This is a different question. While you're thinking of your answer, remember this—the gift that costs the most isn't always the best gift. The best gift is the one that you thought about, the gift that you put the most into. It's something personal, a small piece of you. If you're a teenage boy, you might be tempted to spend all your dough on that girlfriend of yours, but remember your mom. Surprise your whole family this year by planning out something really great to give to show your love. Be around more, put down your phone, get out some board games, slow down a bit, and give the gift that people will remember—the gift of you. Doing this will show your family that you love them. Do it even when you don't feel like it. But be careful, this kind of giving is contagious.

Open Up Your Treasure

Three wise men took off chasing a star across the planet until it came to rest above Jesus' house. Matthew 2:11 says, "On coming to the house, they saw the child with his mother Mary, and they bowed down and worshiped him. Then they opened their treasures and presented him with gifts of gold and of incense and of myrrh." So begins the tradition of gift giving at Christmas. And who better to give the first gift to than Jesus. These wise men brought, what seems to be, their best gifts. In fact, the gifts are described as being "their treasures." A treasure is something that has tremendous value to you. These wise men willingly opened up their treasures for Jesus. God is beckoning us to open our treasure up to Christ, that which we value. He wants us to keep our way pure, raise our children dedicated to the Lord, or give Him our most valuable time or our wisdom as we teach. Our marriage should be opened up to Jesus, our future, our wealth or our poverty. As we open our treasures to Christ, we are making Jesus Lord of our heart; we are making Him more important than the things that are important to us. And that is the gift we bring.

Recognize Christ

Have you ever had someone come up to you and say, "Hey, remember me?" Have you ever responded, "Umm, ya, oh ya, bro, how are you?" when really you were having a hard time recognizing the person? In Luke 2, Jesus arrived on the planet, and some recognized who He was, even as a baby. They had never seen Him before, but God still revealed Christ to them. It says in Luke 2:36-38 that a prophetess named Anna who lived at the temple day and night recognized Jesus. It says "She gave thanks to God and spoke about the child to all who were looking forward to the redemption of Jerusalem" (v.38). This woman did not miss Christ, but she recognized Him. Did you notice where she was? She was in the temple, the Lord's house. Sometimes we miss Christ. He shows up in many ways in our life, but do we recognize Him? Many will miss Christ, even looking right at Him. They will not notice the signs. There may be a star above the house, but maybe these folks are not around God's house enough. The signs of God's gift to us are all around us. Be like Anna. Learn to recognize Christ. Point Him out and tell others. Speak about Him to those who will listen. Help others see too.

Peter Gets It

In Matthew 16, Jesus asked the disciples who the people said that the Son of Man was. The disciples told Him that some said He was John the Baptist, or Elijah, or Jeremiah. Then Jesus asked them, "Who do you say I am?" (v. 15). Now Jesus had just finished walking on water and feeding 4,000 with a few small fish, so this was a big question. Well, Simon piped in, "You are the Christ, the Son of the living God" (v. 16). Simon got something that others weren't getting. Here's Jesus, walking on water and healing people and teaching a message that was blowing modern wisdom out of the water, yet not everyone was getting who He really was. But Simon was. At this recognition, Jesus changed Simon's name to Peter, and told Peter that He was giving him keys to the Kingdom of Heaven, to prayer, and a destiny to build the church. Wow. You see, when you get a revelation of who Christ is, you unlock your future. Jesus begins to redefine you into who you were created to be, and what you were created to do. You are not who everyone else says you are, and you are not what you do, but you are who God says you are, and you can do what God says you can do.

Life to the World

Have you ever noticed in the Scripture that God is always giving? "For God so loved...that He gave..." (John 3:16), or consider John 6:33, "For the bread of God is he who comes down from heaven and gives life to the world." You see, God sent Jesus, who is the Bread, to give life. God is the giver of life. God did not bring death. Man brought death when he ate the fruit. So what was God's answer to death? To give life. Now this life is for any area in you that needs life. How about your body? Finances, or a relationship? A broken heart? Jesus came to bind up the broken heart, to bring life. He's the bread of life. And more of that Bread in you means more life. God, the ultimate giver, has worked very hard to give you life. So dig into the Bread of life and give thanks for the gifts He is giving you.

Life Better for Now and Later

When Jesus walked the earth, He healed and helped many. What was He doing? He was making life better for those who were living. Jesus makes life better for us in two ways. First, He makes life better for us by removing the sting of death. Now, we can look forward to heaven, streets of gold, and the sweet by-and-by. But also notice that He makes life better for us, even while we are currently living. To the blind man Jesus did not say, "Oh don't worry about not being able to see, it will all be better later when you get to glory land." No, He said, "Eyes, be opened." He made life better for us while we are still on earth. Consider what it says in Psalm 107:20: "He sent forth his word and healed them." God gave us the gift of Jesus to make things better now and later. You don't have to wait for the sweet by-and-by to have joy. Pray and ask God today for what you need. He will meet all of your needs according to His riches in glory.

A Christmas Ditty

There once was boy named Toby
Who couldn't wait for Christmas Eve.
He didn't ask anyone for clothes,
He had a list of gifts to achieve.
Like mountains of candy,
Toys, games, and he,
Wished for a brand new Ferrari with keys,
Xbox 360, PlayStation3, 300 vids and three Wii's
iPod, iPhone, iPad, iMac, and any other I's if you please
A book from his mother
A nook from his brother
And four somewhat questionable movies.
So many gifts to list and appraise
No time for chores or dinner,
Toby avoided turkey and mayonnaise
And found himself getting much thinner.
No time for work, no time for family,
There are so many things that I need.
Can't go to school or study today
My life's only time for some greed.
But poor little Toby
Got much so much more when he
Prayed at His church on His knees,
The gift of God's Son

Jesus Christ who has won
And had come to set Toby free.
Although he still plays
and still hates mayonnaise,
Toby has stopped asking for everything he sees.
Now it's time with his mommy
Or drawing with Tommy
He found it's better to give than receive.

Know When to Fold 'Em

When Jesus arrived on the planet, angels sang, treasures were given, and then suddenly, King Herod decided to kill Jesus. What? Jesus just arrived and already they wanted Him dead. In Matthew 2, an angel appeared to Joseph in a dream. "'Get up,' he said, 'take the child and his mother and escape to Egypt'" (v. 13). So Joseph did. You see, God was keeping them safe. God was the solution to the problem that was facing them. You will have some King Herods in your life. When you are in a position to make a huge impact for God, the darkness is not going to be too happy about your light; you set out to do something good, and along comes trouble. But what we learn from this story is that God has a solution for you. The answer came to Joseph as he slept. So relax, don't stress out, take a deep breath, get some sleep even. You do the possible; let God handle the rest.

Why Sing?

Mary was told by the angel that she was going to give birth to the Christ, and that Elizabeth, her relative, was going to have a baby too. Mary went to visit Elizabeth, and when they saw each other, Mary spontaneously burst into a song. It was like a scene from a musical or something. I don't know about you, but I have never been chatting with my brother and then began to sing a song. But Mary did. Then later Zechariah, Elizabeth's husband, started singing too. When the baby Jesus was born, the angels were singing. I'm seeing a trend here. It's important to praise God in song. Why? Just like Mary, you have the seed of God in you. You are highly favored, blessed of God, a child of the King. All of that is reason enough to sing. If you're not feeling it today, maybe that's because you ain't tried singing it.

A Running Theme

As we celebrate Christmas and remember the day that Jesus came into the world as a man, we should remember His message. Just after starting His ministry, Jesus set up the platform He stood for in the famous Sermon on the Mount. In it, He said things like forgive your brother, be meek, pray for your enemies, and if someone asks you for some orange juice (I'm paraphrasing here), give him the whole bottle. Now we can't cover the whole message in a minute, but we can summarize it with a passage found in John 15:12: "My command is this: Love each other as I have loved you." So how did Christ love us? Well, He was willing to give up everything for us. Let's try that this week—I mean really try. Husbands, lay down your life for your wife, for your children. Wives, you too. Let's all slow down a bit this week and remember the gift we can give Jesus is to really show our love to Him by loving each other. In that same teaching, Jesus told us that if we loved Him, we would obey His command (John 14:15). And what was His command? Ah yes, love each other. I'm not saying it's easy, but I can promise you what Jesus promised—it will lead to life.

The Gift that Keeps on Giving

Did you know that Jesus put you in something like the Jelly of the Month Club? He's given you a gift that keeps on giving the whole year through. In John 14, Jesus had come to the earth, ministered, healed, raised the dead, and now He's telling His disciples that He has to go. Here is what He says will happen after He goes... "And I will ask the Father, and he will give you another Counselor to be with you forever—the Spirit of truth" (v. 16-17). He goes on to explain about the Holy Spirit. This is the same Spirit that was poured out in Acts 2. The Holy Spirit brings many gifts to your life. You see, He's the gift that keeps on giving. The Holy Spirit is our counselor, our comforter, and can lead us into truth. The Holy Spirit quickens our mortal bodies and cries out to God, "Abba Father." And Jesus said in Luke 11:13, "How much more will the Father give the Holy Spirit to those who ask him." Well, I don't know what you asked for for Christmas, but if you haven't already, you may just want to ask for the Gift that keeps on giving the whole year round.

Give Him the Best

When you go to church, what do you bring God? In Malachi 1, God was angry because the gifts the people were bringing to Him were the leftovers and garbage of the land. For instance, instead of giving to God the best of their herds, they were giving Him blind and crippled animals. I think sometimes we do the same thing. When we go to God's house, we need to offer our very best. Our best service, and our best treasure. What do you value? We should give it to God first, not last. You see, the more we put God first, the more He can bless us. I'm not just talking about giving the first of our money, though we should. I'm also talking about giving God the best part of our time, the best part of our talents, and the best part of our devotion. So the next time you are giving a gift to God, ask yourself, *Would I give this gift to someone I really love? Is this my best? Would I like getting this as a gift?* For all God has done for us, He deserves nothing less than our best every time.

Another Beginning

Christmas has me reflecting a bit on the change Christ brings to us. Think about it, a year is ending and a new year is beginning. Christ changed everything. He only spent a few years on earth teaching and ministering, yet the world continues to expand the message He spoke. There are more believers today than there were 100 years ago, or 1000 years ago. The message He gave is so large that the whole world stands up and recognizes Christmas, whether they want to or not. His life, death, and resurrection brought us new life. A new day, a new season for all of mankind. In the same way a new year brings a new start to the calendar, Christ brings a fresh start to our lives. He brings hope for tomorrow. He has made us a brand new creation; old things have passed away. Paul teaches us to forget the past and press on to the future. I'm not sure what your year has been filled with, some victories, some crash and burns, maybe some tragedy, and some moments of great happiness. Let's face forward together, let's join hands and march into the unknown future strong with expectations of glory; with God at the helm, we know that nothing is impossible.

Working for Da Man

My first job was mopping floors at Dunkin Donuts. Well, on the first day I mopped, my boss was mad because I stunk it up at mopping. He was yelling at me. He said, "Did you even do what I told you?" Well, when he wasn't around I mouthing off about what I thought of him, *if you know what I mean*. So what's the big deal about that? First Timothy 6:1 says, "All who are under a yoke of slavery should consider their masters worthy of full respect, so that God's name and our teaching may not be slandered." Most of us work for somebody, and here God is telling us that He wants us to give that person full respect. I wasn't giving full respect was I? Now, it didn't say to give full respect because they are a good boss or a respectable person. The respect I was to give was to be a **gift** from me. Why was I supposed to give this gift? Well, because God said so. And God is worthy of respect. This respect becomes a testimony to others of the different life and attitude we as Christians have chosen, and that is to love.

Haven't You Read?

In Matthew 12, the Pharisees complained to Jesus "Look! Your disciples are doing what is unlawful on the Sabbath" (v. 2). Jesus answered, "Haven't you read what David did when he and his companions were hungry?" (v. 3). Now maybe they had never read what David did. Maybe they skipped that chapter in the Bible. Have we read the passage Jesus was talking about? Maybe not… Or if we have read it, do we remember it or were we half asleep or distracted when we were reading it? Jesus was telling the Pharisees that the answer to their question was available to them, they just needed to read the Word to find the answer. It's the same today. Have we read? Have we read the stories in the Word? The Pharisees missed Jesus by failing to read… or maybe they just failed to understand or they forgot what they read. I don't want to miss out on Jesus and all that He has done for me. What an amazing book we have at our fingertips, so many answers, so much knowledge and wisdom. All truth is in the Bible. Let's be people who read, understand and remember.

Fruity Trees

You are called by God to love everyone. And yes, that includes the people you don't like. But here's the thing, loving everyone doesn't mean you have to be willing to go into business with just anyone. It doesn't mean you have to make everyone your best friend and go to the movies with them. It doesn't mean that just anyone can babysit your children. Love isn't the same as trust. There are people who common sense will tell me not to let deep into my world. There were people who asked to follow Jesus in His travels and He would deny them that privilege. Jesus gave us a key to help us discern good people from bad. He says in Matthew 12:33, "Make a tree good and its fruit will be good, or make a tree bad and its fruit will be bad, for a tree is recognized by its fruit." Fruit refers to what a person has produced. Sometimes we meet someone new and we might be tempted to say, "Oh yeah, perfect a new friend, let's invest together, or let's get married, or let's be best friends." Slow down. Remember Jesus' advice. Let's check out the fruit for a second.

High Time

A famous story tells of the inventor of the telephone, Alexander Graham Bell, who filed for the patent for the telephone only a few hours before Elisha Gray. Sorry Elisha… bad timing. Ask a farmer if he can plant in any season and he will tell you no. If you don't plant at the right time, nothing will grow. In John 7:6, Jesus was asked when He was going to the feast in Judea. Jesus said, "The right time for me has not yet come; for you any time is right." Jesus' reply tells us that timing is critical. Think about it, many wanted to kill Jesus throughout His ministry, but Jesus was crucified on exactly the right night, the night of preparation for the Passover lamb, fulfilling the picture that Jesus is our Passover Lamb. Timing is everything. Jesus taught us to be wise like a snake. Before a snake will strike, it will find the exact position and be fully prepared, coiled, and ready, then the snake will strike decisively. Now we're not snakes, but Jesus was teaching us to take the time to be prepared for what we are doing, to get in the right position, and then to act decisively. There is something God has been telling us to start or finish, let's find Jesus' timing.

That Living Feeling

Jesus said in John 6:63-64, "The words I have spoken to you are spirit and they are life. Yet there are some of you who do not believe." You see, when you get around truth, when you get around the Spirit of God, you will feel life. Something inside of you is saying, "I want more of *that*." Christ's words are alive. They live on today, still full of power—power to change this planet. And when we hear them, somewhere deep in the depths of who we are, we feel this message resonating in our being. Life. These living words bring even the dark and stagnant parts of us to life; desires in our heart that have been dormant are nudged, stirred, moved. Even right now, there is a stirring inside. Life. This life that Christ has given is inside us, and others will feel it when we speak truth. They will be drawn to us, something about us makes them feel alive. It's contagious and it's relentless. The Bible isn't just some history book; it's a book full of words that will bring you the life God desires you to have. You are a spirit, and your spirit needs the Word of God.

Happy Holidays

Have you noticed the trend to take the word "Christ" out of Christmas? I see the words "Happy Holidays" all over the place. But here's some good news about that. "Holiday" is taken from the phrase "Holy Day." "Holy" means to be set apart for God's plans and purposes. So now all over the world, we are announcing a joyful set of days dedicated to God. So hey, Jesus still wins! Even so, if we want to ensure that Christ stays in Christmas, the best way to do that is just to get more Jesus into the hearts of the people. God showed tremendous wisdom by sending Jesus into our lives. He showed us that the world cannot be changed by bringing a bunch of rules down from the mountain; the world is only changed by getting the seed of God into the hearts of man. You see, God is changing us from the inside out. And if we want to change the world, it also happens from the inside out. We shouldn't be surprised when the world does things we don't agree with. They don't know any better. Telling them the rules may not help, but giving them the seed of Jesus Christ, now that is the key to change.

Get This Place Cleaned Up

There's wrapping paper all over the floor, stuff strewn, food left out, I've got my pajamas on, I'm un-shaven, un-ready, half asleep—it's time to get this place cleaned up. The house is a mess. You know, you and I can get a little like that house sometimes. Second Timothy 2:20-21 says, "In a large house there are articles not only of gold and silver, but also of wood and clay; some are for special purposes and some for ignoble. If a man cleanses himself from the latter, he will be an instrument for noble purposes, made holy, useful to the Master and prepared to do any good work." Sure, your house has some messy stuff in it. Mine does too. This doesn't make your house bad. You just need to take out the trash, is all. And the more trash we cleanse ourselves of, the more work we get to do. That may not sound like fun, but if the work comes from God, you can bet it will be fun. He's not in the business of making you miserable for serving Him. If you ask, Jesus, the Word of God, will help you clean up. In fact, there is no better cleaner than the Word of God. It's like nuclear powered PineSol.

Come Say What Happens

When God speaks, stuff happens. If He says "Let there be," get ready for something big to happen. Scientists call it a big bang. That's putting it lightly. As Jesus walked the earth, we saw the same power in His words. He came to this earth as a man, and yet He would tell storms to quiet down, He would tell Satan to go away, He would tell crippled people to get up and walk, His words were powerful. Now we are brothers of Christ, adopted sons of God. We were made in the likeness and image of God, and Jesus said we would do greater stuff than we saw Him do. He gives us His Spirit, the same Spirit that raised Christ from the dead. So with all that in mind, what kind of things are we saying? Does God just want us describing how things are? If that's the case, God wouldn't have said "Let there be light." He would have said, "Man, it's pretty dark around here." And Jesus might have said to the storm, "Hope this boat doesn't sink." Instead they spoke what they wanted to happen, not what was happening. God wants us to be godly. So let's try adding this discipline to our lives.

Recognize the Answer

In the Bible, we read the story of a couple, Zechariah and Elizabeth, who wanted to have a kid. So they prayed and asked God for a child. Well, in Luke 1:13, an angel showed up to talk to Zechariah, which is pretty cool all by itself, but then the angel said, "Your prayer has been heard. Your wife Elizabeth will bear you a son, and you are to give him the name John." This was the announcement that John the Baptist was coming. But you know what... even though Zechariah had prayed for this and even though the angel was telling him it was going to happen, Zechariah didn't believe it. As a result, the angel made it so Zechariah couldn't talk until the baby was born. Our words have power. Sometimes we pray for something, and then when the answer finally comes and that answer from God is staring us right in the face, we miss it. We don't believe. It happened to Zechariah, and it may happen to you. God answered Zechariah's prayer in His timing. The answer came at the exact right time. God has heard you, as well. You are a child of the King. The answer may be staring you in the face right now. Just believe.

God's Will

Paul was telling the Colossian church how thankful he was for them because they were keeping a strong faith and growing in love. He said in Colossians 1:9, "For this reason...we have not stopped praying for you and asking God to fill you with the knowledge of his will through all spiritual wisdom and understanding." Ah yes, the will of God. God has a will for you. When you have a decision to make, knowing His will is critical. Should I move? Should I change jobs? Who should I marry? We can see from this scripture that the knowledge of God's will comes to you through **spiritual wisdom**. Spiritual wisdom is wisdom about spiritual things, invisible things, things like faith and love. Both are invisible. Hebrews 11 tells us that faith is the substance of things hoped for, the evidence of things unseen. God is love, and God is unseen. Does God want you to know His will? Sure He does, but it's hard to see His will when we look at problems or circumstances. Since God is Spirit, that is where the power is, so stop looking at the physical world for a second, pray, and ask God to show you His will.

Blow the Trumpet

Joel 2:1 says, "Blow the trumpet in Zion." Well, I don't play the trumpet and even if I did, I live in Mesa. Where is Zion? When Israel was attacked by an enemy, the trumpet would the signal Israel's army to assemble and get ready for battle. So what does that have to do with Zion? First, you need to know that Zion is not just a city from the Matrix movie, but it is spoken of in the Word as the city of God. God is telling you that when things are going wrong and you are pretty sure you are losing the battle, you can call on God's help, and His army will assemble and fight the battle for you. Your mess may seem pretty big, but God and His armies aren't about to lose. You should know that you don't have to be able to play an actual trumpet either; prayer will call in the big guns. Prayer is your trumpet. I get myself in a mess every now and then, and thankfully, God in His mercy comes to my aid every time. Are you in a mess? Get out your trumpet.

Go Ahead—Praise!

In Psalm 150:6 David sings, "Let everything that has breath praise the LORD." David, being a man after God's own heart, is a guy we can learn from. Sometimes guys think that singing is wimpy, but David was warrior. Think Mel Gibson in *Braveheart*. David led his armies to battle and in wars, he was acclaimed for having defeated tens of thousands of men. Even as a teenager, he tore up a big guy named Goliath when he popped him in the head with a stone, then cut off his head. David was passionate about life and about praising God, which is why he would have written something like, "Let everything that has breath praise the LORD." Are you breathing today? Then take opportunities to praise God for whatever He's done for you. Really talk to Him. Really praise Him. And when everyone is singing in church, really focus on the words and what you are singing to God and make your praise personal. Your heavenly Father loves you, and He has given you the breath you are breathing. So Praise God. Sing songs, hymns, and spiritual songs in your heart to the Lord. God doesn't have to be some distant ruler in your life anymore. Jesus has made a way for you to get up close and personal with the Father.

About the Author

 Jason Anderson serves as Executive Pastor of Living Word Bible Church in Mesa, Arizona. Living Word Bible Church is the 12ᵗʰ fastest growing church in America. He is an evangelist, leading to Christ crowds of over 50,000 in nations such as Thailand, Cambodia, and India. He is the first man in modern history to preach the gospel in Vietnam at a publicly advertised event where an estimated 10,000 received Christ. He has written church leadership curriculum that is currently taught at college level, teaches and ministers all over the world and is also the voice of nationally syndicated radio show *Taking A Minute*, which airs in over 200 cities. Married in 1992, Jason Anderson has four beautiful children.

Prayer of Salvation

God loves you—no matter who you are, no matter what your past. God loves you so much that He gave His one and only begotten Son for you. The Bible tells us that "...whoever believes in him shall not perish but have eternal life" (John 3:16 NIV). Jesus laid down His life and rose again so that we could spend eternity with Him in heaven and experience His absolute best on earth. If you would like to receive Jesus into your life, say the following prayer out loud and mean it from your heart.

Heavenly Father, I come to You now, admitting that I am a sinner Right now I choose to turn away from sin, and I ask You to cleanse me of all unrighteousness. I believe that Your Son, Jesus, died on the cross to take away my sins. I also believe that He rose again from the dead so that I might be forgiven of my sins and made righteous through faith in Him. I call upon the name of Jesus Christ to be the Savior and Lord of my life. Jesus, I choose to follow You and ask that You fill me with the power of the Holy Spirit. I declare that right now, I am a child of God. I am free from sin and full of the righteousness of God. I am saved in Jesus' name. Amen.

If you prayed this prayer to receive Jesus Christ as your Savior for the first time, please contact us on the Web at **www.harrisonhouse.com** to receive a free book.

Or you may write to us at

Harrison House
P.O. Box 35035
Tulsa, Oklahoma 74153

The Harrison House Vision

Proclaiming the truth and the power

Of the Gospel of Jesus Christ

With excellence;

Challenging Christians to

Live victoriously,

Grow spiritually,

Know God intimately.

Fast. Easy. Convenient.

For the latest Harrison House product information and author news, look no further than your computer. All the details on our powerful, life-changing products are just a click away. New releases, E-mail subscriptions, Podcasts, testimonies, monthly specials—find it all in one place. Visit harrisonhouse.com today!

harrisonhouse

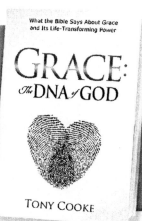